What Financial Advisors Say about *A Matter of Time—*

"*A Matter of Time* is absolutely fantastic! I just wish I had it ten years ago when I started my practice."

Anton Diedericks,
CFP®, WellAdvised Financial Advisors, Hobart, Australia

"I liked how this book was divided into a *why* hourly and then *how* to make it successful. Personally, since I'm sold on the why already, I found the how part to be very informative and instructional. I like how the book discusses operations, revenue, profitability, scalability, all the types of things firm owners need to consider. I think this book will serve as a resource for those of us who are already in the industry or those who are pursuing the hourly model."

Feraud Calixte,
JD, CFP®, Vantage Pointe Planning, Burlington, NC

"I can't tell you how much I enjoyed this book. It is clear and concise and contains very valuable information. It's going to help me as I take another look at my practice and decide how to proceed from here. I'm feeling some changes are in order. When I started, there were no hourly planners. It was completely unheard of. We now have no openings for new clients and we are desperate to have someone to refer prospects. I guess a trail has been blazed! Thank you for taking the time and effort to write this book. It is much needed."

Debbra Dillon,
CFP®, Dillon Financial Planning, Inc., Eagle, ID

A MATTER
OF
TIME

Principles, Myths & Methods
for the Hourly Financial Advisor

Mark Berg, CFP® &
Matthew Jackson, CFA®

ISBN
   Hard Cover: 978-1-7375766-0-0
   Paperback: 978-1-7375766-1-7
   eBook: 978-1-7375766-2-4
   Audiobook: 978-1-7375766-3-1

Published by Peak 2. Please visit www.hourlyexchange.com for more information.

"Genius, at a technical level, is the modality combining the farsightedness needed to deduce the existence of a higher peak with the character and ability to survive the punishing journey to higher ground."

"Excellence," Eric Weinstein, *Edge.org*, 2013

Contents

Part 1: Foundations

Part 2: Serving the Client

Part 3: Running the Firm

Authors' Note

These are exciting times to be a financial planner. As compared to the beginnings of other professional services like accounting (1887), psychology (1879), law (as early as 50 AD), and medicine (2700 BC), we are truly in the formative years of our own. Just as each of these professions went through decades, even centuries of evolution to arrive at where they are today, so must we.

In the early years, access to the best professionals was often restricted. As the profession has become more mainstream, services are becoming available for all, but not without a struggle.

I (Mark) have been an hourly practitioner since 2000, and I have seen and experienced this struggle firsthand. It is as if there are invisible forces (I call them myths) holding us back from having thriving, profitable firms that provide access to high-quality planning advice for the millions who can't access these services today. Our goal in writing this book is to help hourly practitioners break free of these myths to create best-in-class firms of the future.

Matthew and I are passionate about this as we believe that the hourly mode of offering financial advice to the consumer is the future of financial advice. Most professional services share this mode in common, with varying hourly rates based on expertise. I have observed a steady increase in demand for hourly planning services, with demand outstripping the current supply, and I firmly believe that we are on the front end of a tsunami of demand.

Therefore, we—a small but growing enclave in the sprawling financial advice industry—must be ready to meet this demand. Our hope is that this book will equip you to either build a healthy planning practice from the ground up, or improve one that you have already built. Together we can help move the current state of our industry toward a future profession.

A special thanks to Matthew, who through gentle persistence helped me lift my gaze from running my own hourly practice and set forth what I describe here as the future of the industry. This book wouldn't exist without him.

Introduction

Running a business in an hourly fashion is only possible for a true expert who can demonstrate value for every dollar. This is why established professions such as law, accounting, and medicine are able to charge explicitly for expertise.

In this book, we set out a case for the hourly model as a viable and attractive option for the professional financial planner of the future.

For the advisor who adopts it, the hourly model offers two unique benefits:

- It is possible to charge for value and demonstrate the value-fee relationship.
- It provides a clear set of internal levers for running the business efficiently.

Today most firms have adopted an assets under management (AUM), retainer, or commission compensation structure, and very few planning firms follow an hourly model. To many observers, it is a baffling choice and will likely remain so.

The book is aimed chiefly at the next generation of planners and founders who are interested in alternative approaches to the two critical issues: value-based pricing and business management. And have a taste for adventure.

We admit that the hourly model is difficult to implement successfully *if you do not know how*. In particular, it is dangerous to follow rules that apply in traditional financial advice firms, but seldom transfer to an hourly context.

The insights contained in this book are based on real-life experiences, acquired over two decades building and running an hourly planning firm (Timothy Financial Counsel), and having to overcome many of the challenges hourly practitioners are likely to encounter.

We hope the book will serve as a starting point for those who are inspired by the challenge of building a future-ready firm. If this is the path you have chosen, welcome and good luck.

PART 1

FOUNDATIONS

Chapter 1

Myths vs. Reality

Myths about the hourly model are many and varied. Why begin the book with them? Because many of the problems that hourly firms face can be traced back to a myth about the hourly model, which the firm's founder has at some point internalized.

This could be the result of a conversation with another planner (everyone has an opinion about the hourly model) or through a self-generated assumption that has never been challenged.

Deprogramming yourself of these myths is the first and potentially most important step on the path to success. If you are new to the hourly model, or considering it as an option, knowing these issues is also an excellent place to start. As we will see later on in chapter 3, there are enough genuine challenges with the hourly model to occupy the mind of a firm owner, without the need for mythical ones.

Myth 1: Hourly fees are only for the middle market.

It is acknowledged that the hourly model makes it possible to give high-quality financial advice to the middle market, or consumers who fall outside the scope of the retiree-oriented, asset-focused advisory firm. However, the benefit is a by-product of the model rather than its *raison d'être*. Hourly advisors are free to serve anyone and everyone.

Although Mark's colleagues serve clients who range from recent college graduates to high net worth individuals ($1m+), Mark's own clients are typically ultra-high net worth ($20m+). As the needs of such individuals are often highly complex, yearly fees for a single client can run into the tens and even hundreds of thousands.

Hourly advisors, in other words, should not confine themselves to targeting clients who are "less well off," or see their role as serving the clients that other advisors don't want.

In fact, focusing on less complex clients exclusively may, in the long run, result in limiting or eliminating the profitability of the firm. The desire to serve the underserved is a worthy goal and can be achieved within the scope of a firm that serves multiple client types at differentiated rates (see chapters 4 and 5 for more details).

The versatility of hourly is one of its greatest strengths, and it should be used to full effect.

Myth 2: Hourly fees discourage existing clients from asking for advice.

The idea here is that charging clients whenever they request advice will make them less likely to do so. Yet people engage in activities every day that they know will incur financial cost. For example, no one questions the fairness of an airline charging for a flight, or a hotel charging for a room. People often look forward to events—such as holidays or weddings—that involve significant financial outlay.

If they don't perceive the value of the exchange (as in the case of parking tickets, late fee payments), this is a different story. But in general, if a service has value, people are willing to exchange money for it.

Clients who see the value of advice will be no more reluctant to pick up the phone than they would be booking an appointment with a personal trainer, hair stylist, or accountant.

Hourly *does* mean that clients are less likely to call simply to pass the time of day, or to ask trivial questions that do not require the advisor's expertise. This arrangement makes the most of your time and your client's money.

Myth 3: Time-tracking is a nightmare to implement.

While setting up an effective time-tracking system is not easy, the actual process of tracking your time need take only ten minutes a day. Even considering the effort to set up and maintain the system, the investment is small considering the potential benefits (more about tracking in chapter 2).

Most financial planners do not have experience in time-tracking, never having been forced to do it. We suspect that the impression of time-tracking as an onerous task comes from observing other professions who are obliged to track time for regulatory reasons.

Lawyers can be expected to document how time is spent in increments as small as six minutes. Yet, somehow, this has not stopped them from wanting to become lawyers. Currently, in fact, many more people want to become lawyers than financial planners.

Financial planners do currently enjoy an advantage over lawyers, in that they are able to track time however they want. As we cover in chapter 9, this approach can and should be thoroughly pragmatic. Furthermore, technology is making the process of time-tracking easier all the time, with dozens of helpful apps to choose from.

Myth 4: Hourly fees make you inaccessible.

Everyone, regardless of pricing model, has the same number of hours in a year as everyone else. The issue is not really one of availability, but *perception* of availability.

It is true that if you do not charge for your time, clients may have the perception of unlimited access to your calendar. This perception will give way to reality when seven clients call you at the same time during a market downturn.

An advisor with no limits on their availability is ultimately less likely to be available. A planner with control over their time, however, is *more* likely to be available. For this reason, hourly planners can and do serve more clients than the typical advisor with a supposedly open door.

One way or another, advisors have to ration their time and get paid for it. Charging by the hour is a logical way of doing that.

Myth 5: You shouldn't bill clients more during stressful life events.

Inevitably there will be difficult, unexpected life occurrences (such as divorce or bereavement) that create a sudden, urgent need for planning support. The worry is that, since the client will be in distress, he or she may feel that the advisor is compounding their woes with a larger-than-average invoice.

It is hard to think of any other provider of a valuable service related to a stressful life event, whether a funeral director or a divorce attorney, who would waive their fees on such grounds. It is precisely *because* they are adding value at a difficult time that their fees are warranted and earned.

If the client really does not feel they should pay, this is an indication that they do not value the service. This is revealed by the stressful event in question, but not caused by it. And it is a sign that the client may be better off with another advisor.

As we cover later, quibbles about fees from clients are the exception rather than the rule. Regular updates and clear setting of expectations up front are normally sufficient to allay any fears about runaway costs.

Myth 6: Hourly is cost-based pricing, not value-based.

Short of picking a number at random, cost-based is the worst way to go about setting prices. A firm's revenues must exceed its costs, to be sure, but simply adding an arbitrary margin to an estimate of cost will *not* reflect the value of an item or service.

Value-based pricing is what every firm should aspire to. For financial planning, and professional services in general, we would argue that charging for time and expertise ($/expert hour) is the *purest* form of value-based pricing.

There is no reason why charging an hourly rate should equate to charging based on cost. Price should reflect a client's willingness to pay, and the client is not aware of the internal costs of the business, how fixed costs are allocated, or how much the advisor is costing the business per hour.

What they are aware of is the expertise of the advisor, the problems they want them to solve, and how available this expertise is elsewhere, if at all.

These factors comprise the client's willingness to pay, which equals the value-based price. The hourly rate should therefore be geared to this willingness to pay, and not to the cost to deliver.

Some advisors go further in their objections to the hourly model, saying that it does not reflect the time and money saved thanks to the advice. These savings can run into the millions in the case of tax-related counsel.

It is true that a customer is buying the benefits and not the product. The producer of the goods is responsible for the product alone and entitled to no more than its market price. In this case, the product is units of time and expertise.

Myth 7: You get paid more when you work inefficiently.

This seems logical: time-based charging incentivizes an advisor to go slower at the client's expense, while the efficient advisor is punished with lower wages. It just doesn't work out that way in practice.

Even if we assume that overcharging clients and being inefficient is your avowed intent, the hourly fee model is probably the worst way to achieve this aim undetected. The need-driven nature of the model dictates that every bill must be tied to an event for which the rationale is clear to both parties.

Clients are much more likely to identify activities that are not valuable to them when they can clearly link advisor effort to fees paid, as is the case with the hourly model. If the client does perceive that time is being spent poorly, it is in their power to terminate the relationship immediately and share their negative experience with others.

Even in the short term, working inefficiently is not in the narrow financial interests of the planner.

Hourly planners typically have more potential clients than they have time for. An hour saved through efficiency with one client, therefore, becomes a chargeable hour that can be used for another. Wasting time is therefore a risk that brings no financial advantage and limits the number of clients you can serve, while potentially putting those relationships at risk.

The long-term commercial incentives for the hourly advisor are toward doing only what is needed, and as quickly as possible. This is what makes it an ideal model for those who want to run an efficient business, as we will see in subsequent chapters.

Myth 8: You charge for your ignorance, but give away knowledge for free.

It can take twenty years to acquire insights that can be communicated in the space of a few billable hours, providing significant value for what appears to be a modest financial reward.

An inexperienced advisor, on the other hand, might take longer to achieve the same result, and so incur more billable hours. Why should a client pay more for less?

If an hourly firm has just one hourly rate for all advisors, regardless of experience, and assigns clients to these advisors at random, regardless of client need, then this myth does indeed hold true.

In reality, planners of differing levels of experience should (and in the case of Timothy Financial do) have different hourly rates that reflect their levels of experience. Clients know it is in their interests to have the best-qualified advisor for their situation. A more experienced advisor may cost more per hour but will be more effective and efficient.

A client whose situation does not require complex expertise will naturally be happy to be served by a resource who costs less per hour.

As for the objection that twenty years of experience cannot be adequately captured by an hour's worth of fees, remember that the hourly premium an experienced advisor can charge applies to all hours billed in a given year.

This combined annual premium adds up to a substantial figure when compared with the earnings of a less experienced advisor.

Knowledge, in other words, is not given away for free.

Myth 9: Hourly planning = passive advice.

The flawed assumption in this myth is that when clients are paying by the hour, initiating meetings and phone calls must be left entirely to the client. In this scenario, the advisor is truly a passive actor, never a proactive one.

It is possible to take a passive approach to hourly planning and simply wait for clients to reach out to you. But this clearly makes for a poor advisory relationship. Rather than taking a purely ad hoc approach, there should be a regular cadence to the relationship (meeting once or twice a year usually makes sense for most clients), which the advisor is responsible for proposing and upholding.

The client must naturally decide whether the proposed meetings actually take place, and some clients may decline invitations if they feel they're in good shape.

Nonetheless, it remains the duty of an advisor to monitor a client's progress and maintain a proactive attitude. Financial planning has no finish line, and so in every conversation, there should always be a suggested next date to reconnect.

The advisor should alert clients by email to important developments (such as tax law changes) if they are likely to be affected by them. General emails to all clients are not charged. Specific emails to individual clients are part of the hourly billing.

"When trust has been established in a relationship, proactive calls or emails are not only appreciated but actually encouraged."

And it is also important to be alert to changes in a client's situation. A client of Mark's once sent some information "for the file," mentioning in passing that he was planning to extend his office lease prior to selling the building. After reading this email, Mark immediately called and asked if the client had thought through the implications of making a ten-year financial commitment, three years out from retirement. The client had not.

In Mark's experience, when trust has been established in a relationship, proactive calls or emails are not only appreciated but actually encouraged. Such clients are pleased to know that their advisor is looking out for them and welcome new planning ideas, whether they decide to pursue them or not.

Myth 10: The hourly model is transactional.

There is a view that the hourly model is inherently transactional in nature—that is to say, best suited to project-based work and one-off interactions.

Viewing yourself as a transactional advisor can be a self-fulfilling prophecy. It is possible to put your head down and simply churn out plans, waving clients on their way to make room for the next one. But this is not a limitation imposed by the fee model. It is more to do with a limited view of financial planning.

The initial work—the financial plan itself, and various quick wins of the form, "If you do x, you will save y"—will not be repeatable and are in fact one-off events.

But as trust builds over time, the value of the advice morphs from quick wins and, "How much money can you save me?" to "I can sleep well at night because I know you have my back and will give me the advice as to x and y and when I need it."

The records of Timothy Financial show that 75% of revenues in a given year come from clients the firm has served in the past, and only 25% from new clients. People within the 75% are engaging at varying levels of frequency, but there is clearly a relationship that has persisted beyond the initial plan.

The real problem with this myth is a false distinction between relational and transactional.

We have plenty of so-called relationships with individuals we also transact with. This includes professionals such as doctors and therapists and other commercial enterprises. If we are failing to build relationships as financial advisors, the fee model is not where the issue lies.

Myth 11: Efficiency is bad for building relationships.

This is a combination of Myth 5 (hourly = inaccessible) and Myth 8 (hourly = transactional). Unlike Myth 9 (hourly = inefficient), the claim here is that efficiency is in fact a bad thing.

According to the logic, if clients are constantly aware that the clock is ticking, the relationship will be reduced to a purely business-focused set of interactions, crowding out the possibility of a more personal connection.

It is true that a good relationship should not be all business. This means that a certain amount of inefficiency, such as social events, conversations about kids, sports, and vacations, can go toward building an effective advisory relationship.

You might think that hourly billing precludes this dimension, but this is, once again, based on a narrow definition of financial advice. The truth is that there are few topics that are more personal and emotional than money.

The more money is involved, the more emotion is typically involved. Accordingly, few fields are more psychologically and emotionally charged than helping people to solve money-related issues.

"An advisor who follows an integrated approach will not only deliver better advice, but also build relational capital."

Take the case of a client who is a co-trustee of her mother's funds. The narrowly defined financial objective may be to maximize risk-adjusted return. Then the client says, "By the way, my mom is deeply attached to the brokerage account, and I think it's going to be hard to persuade her to withdraw money from it."

Suddenly, you are party to some highly personal information, which happens also to be highly relevant in reaching an effective solution.

If an advisor were to confine the discussion to financial topics alone, treating the problems as purely technical, important issues are going to be missed, and solutions left unimplemented.

An advisor who follows an integrated approach will not only deliver better advice, but also build relational capital via the nonfinancial aspects of financial issues. The goal of a relationship is not pursued, but naturally ensues.

Myth 12: You can't scale a business with this model.

As with many other myths, this applies to suboptimally managed firms, but not to all hourly firms.

Other professions that charge by the hour are among the most lucrative in the world, usually many times larger than the typical planning firm. The reason is easily demonstrable from fundamentals. If you can turn your time into money, profitability—and therefore future growth—becomes a question of how much you charge per hour, your utilization rate, and your cost base.

Taking a simple example: a solo advisor who charges $450 per hour and advises 1,000 hours per year (~50% utilization), stands to make $450,000 per year.

> "Other professions that charge by the hour are among the most lucrative in the world, usually many times larger than the typical planning firm."

Theoretically, there is no upper limit on the amount per hour that can be charged. We know from the legal profession that hourly rates can be in the thousands. In other words, there is no *prima facie* reason to assume that hourly billing is any less profitable than the other approaches.

The question of the scalability of the hourly model is dealt with in more detail in chapters 7 through 9. But the short answer is yes it does scale, better than other models, and may in fact be the only type of financial planning firm that can truly scale.

In summary, if you genuinely understand these myths and how they can affect your thinking, you will run a profitable and successful hourly firm. The remainder of the book is essentially a series of footnotes to the thoughts expressed in this chapter. That said, the devil is in the detail, so we invite you to stay with us as we journey on.

Chapter 2

The Upsides of Hourly

There are so many benefits to the hourly model, it is a challenge to fit them all in one chapter. As mentioned in the introduction, there are two dimensions to the hourly approach: how you price the service, and how you run the firm. This dichotomy is most commonly described in terms of working "in" versus working "on" the business.

In this chapter, we look at the benefits from the perspective of both dimensions.

Client-facing Benefits ("in the business")

Offering: As the hourly model tends naturally to promote efficiency, it brings into greater focus *who* needs *what* and *how much*. Knowing these details allows you to segment clients and design propositions intentionally.

Pricing: Hourly pricing is arguably the most logical way to price a professional service. Furthermore, it is robust (in other words, against market shocks) in the short term, and defensible (from client/regulator scrutiny) in the long term.

Communication: The simplicity of the hourly approach can be a liability if mishandled but, if communicated well, has the potential to reinforce perception of value and willingness to pay.

Internal ("on the business")

Measurement: Time-tracking is vital for recording billable hours. But in addition to billing, it is also a business tool, providing transparency into how work is delivered and how time is spent on nonbillable activities.

Management: With a high-resolution view of how staff are spending their time, it is possible not only to identify problems impacting capacity and efficiency, but to solve them by setting quantifiable goals and tracking progress toward them with precision.

Planning: In the pursuit of a long-term vision, leaders may need to pivot into new territory and create time for new activities (such as mentoring, training). These activities need not disrupt the business if grounded in an understanding of what is possible.

Let's take a look at each of the benefits outlined here in more detail.

Offering

In the advice world today, many different services fall under the umbrella term of *financial planning*.

Medical professionals are much more precise about delineating different fields (such specialties as oncology, pediatrics, cardiology) and different procedures within those fields (for example, tumor removal, appendectomy, coronary bypass).

This clarity is obviously important for the end user, but it is also vital for progress in medical science. A common vocabulary provides a basis for experts to discuss and refine procedures for diagnosis and treatment.

In financial planning, this would seem to imply that we should be aiming for more tightly defined advice offerings, with fixed-service levels, modules, and packages.

A Tailored Solution

At first glance, however, hourly appears to be taking us away from a clearly defined offering. The very notion of hourly sounds noncommittal and shapeless.

The case for retaining the flexibility of an hourly model, however, is that financial planning is truly about planning for life. Everyone's life story is different, and life in general is unpredictable.

All planners are aware that presenting a financial plan to the client is not the end of the planning process, but the end of the beginning. Children get married, couples get divorced, people retire, a partner dies, Aunt Gertrude dies and leaves a huge estate (you should be so lucky), relatives get sick, and spouses get fired or promoted. A financial planning relationship has to absorb all of these shocks, and the value line is jagged, not neat and linear.

This is a good argument in favor of a model that can adapt to the limitless contours of life's landscape.

A Coherent Proposition

Although it may appear shapeless, the hourly approach is the best way to create a truly coherent service offering. It is predicated on the idea that the value of financial advice is a function of time and expertise. Just as DNA is the substrate of human life, units of time and expertise are the building blocks of a financial planning proposition.

Tracking client relationships by time and resource gives the planner an extremely detailed portrait of the financial planning relationship. Everything can be described both qualitatively (what was done) and quantitatively (how much was done).

For a given planning event—such as a divorce, or the birth or death of a loved one—an hourly planner must clearly define who and what is involved in delivering the solution (otherwise, they cannot price it).

This practice is already common in the legal profession. If the quantity unit (number of hours) represents the effort, and the fee unit ($/hour) reflects the expertise required, these two combine to make the final price.

This higher level of resolution creates greater clarity than currently exists in mainstream financial advice. Planners typically have no comparable data that describe the relationship between the many different types of planning engagement and the fees charged. It is only possible to create such a dataset by having a crystal-clear understanding of what is involved in a given engagement, and the vocabulary to describe it.

> "We can never standardize life, and so it must be the circumstances of each individual that determine the final price."

This might imply that the next step is to create fixed-service packages and modules. There is a case to be made for this approach, but there is also a caveat. While data can be aggregated across firms and engagements in order to synthesize needs-based packages, the "average client" is rarely seen in the wild.

While our understanding of what is required to perform certain procedures will improve over time, no two life events are the same and may differ considerably from individual to individual.

We can standardize procedures and terminology, but we can never standardize life, and so it must be the circumstances of each individual that determine the final price.

Pricing

The fee model debate in the financial advice space is unending, and there are arguments in favor of every model. For you, a business owner, there is ultimately only one question that matters: what will the client accept?

For a fee to be acceptable, it must fulfill two conditions:

1. The client can afford the fee (**ability to pay**).
2. The client believes the fee is worth it (**willingness to pay**).

Ability to Pay

When considering ability to pay, the advantage of the hourly model is clear. Most financial advisors filter out nonliquid, nonwealthy, or nondelegator prospects who constitute the majority of the population.

The hourly planner, on the other hand, is in the same situation as an attorney or a CPA. Anyone who is not living from paycheck to paycheck has access, which creates a much larger potential market for financial advice.

> "Willingness to pay is *not* the issue.
>
> The problem is unwillingness to charge."

Willingness to Pay

If clients were not prepared to pay for financial advice by the hour, there would be no hourly firms. And if people were, in general, not prepared to pay by the hour for anything, there would be no legal or accounting firms.

Willingness to pay is *not* the issue. The issue is that, compared with other professions, there are so few hourly planners to meet the demand. In other words, the problem is unwillingness to charge.

Resilience

Unlike firms whose revenues are linked to the vagaries of the stock market, the hourly planner is more or less fully shielded from these external shocks. Being insulated in this way means less anxiety about the S&P or the Dow, and a greater ability to plan.

Furthermore, demand for advisor time typically increases when markets suddenly decline.

At the same time that other firms face a combination of higher workloads, static costs, and fixed or declining revenues, hourly advisors see revenues increase in line with effort.

Sustainability

The hourly model—paying for someone's time and expertise—is arguably the oldest of all pricing models, going back thousands of years to the dawn of commerce.

Lindy's Law, popularized by Nassim Taleb, stipulates that the life expectancy of ideas or technologies increases in proportion with age. A book that is still read after a thousand years has a longer "life expectancy" than an airport thriller that came out last week.

On this basis, we would expect hourly to outlast all other models. While other advisors must worry about regulation, competition, and client tastes, the hourly planner can rest comfortably in the knowledge that hourly fees will remain valid for millennia.

Communication

Communication is the process of demonstrating the link between the value delivered and fees charged. The art of communication is so powerful that it can be used to create the appearance of value where little or none exists. Poor communication achieves the opposite result.

When it comes to communicating value, the price we charge for a service is as important as the words we use to describe it. As stated earlier, the hourly model computes value as a function of time and expertise. As this is an easy concept to grasp, the hourly planner will have no difficulty explaining the link between fees and value.

You can appeal to intuitive concepts such as amount of activity (big project = more tasks/steps = more time), and/or complexity (more complexity = more issues = greater expertise required).

Unlike some fee discussions, which rely more on trust than transparency, the very transparency of the hourly model engenders trust, as the planner who uses it clearly has nothing to hide.

> "The hourly model computes value as a function of time and expertise."

Measurement

If you want to charge by the hour and be successful, comprehensive time-tracking is highly advisable. That is, all members of the firm classify all their activities, both billable and nonbillable, by category of task and time spent.

Client-side

In tracking how much time is spent on a given activity, and by whom, you can identify if the amount of time and expertise spent on a specific client is appropriate. Simple as this may seem, it is hard to be accurate, let alone precise, without consistent measurement.

While many advice firms have a vague notion that some clients take up a great deal of time while others may not be receiving enough attention, the planner who tracks time has actual data, down to the minute.

Business-side

In addition to shining a light on the client relationship, comprehensive time-tracking allows a business to shine a light on its own internal workings.

This is a real opportunity, as the human brain is typically poor at estimating time allocation without assistance. Anyone who begins to track their time in this way will find out quickly that they are more likely to overestimate productivity than underestimate it.

The transparency of having real data about your business is a manifold blessing. It provides a bird's-eye view of how time is being spent at a global level. For example, how much time is devoted to administrative overhead versus business development.

It also works at an employee level. It may be the case that one employee is unusually slow or fast at a certain category of task, or devoting an unusual amount of time to a certain activity. This may not be a problem (if the role is specialized, for instance), but it should not ideally be a surprise.

By measuring how time and expertise is being used and where it is being spent, an owner can detect the symptoms of an issue before it becomes chronic.

Management

If the aim of measurement is to enable transparency, the primary target of management is to leverage transparency to achieve efficiency. Greater efficiency in a firm means greater capacity, which in turn leads to higher growth and/or profitability.

Advancing from measurement to management is a matter of having a clear view as to how things should be done. This means having precise key performance indicators (KPIs) that reveal how far away a process or team is from performing its role in an optimal manner.

Inefficiency may arise from a specific individual's attitude—for example, a skilled advisor who hoards routine tasks that can and should be delegated. Such an employee could be given a set of personal KPIs that incentivize a certain split of activities more reflective of their expertise.

It is also possible for processes, rather than individuals, to be inefficient, putting pressure on multiple team members at once. Analysis might reveal that client onboarding is a major bottleneck. In this case, a manager could first investigate whether difficulty does indeed arise from the process, or if more staff are needed.

> "In some cases, simply identifying the issue and measuring it can be enough to make the process go faster."

If the process is found to be at fault, it can be amended, and the target of onboarding time adjusted accordingly. In some cases, simply identifying the issue and measuring it can be enough to make the process go faster. This is a basic form of gamification: when the brain has something to aim at, it is automatically motivated to perform.

Planning

In his book *The E Myth*, Michael Gerber sets out three distinct personas that inhabit every business (and businessperson):

- The technician (who does the work of the business)
- The manager (who makes the business work)
- The entrepreneur (who creates and updates the business)

Financial advice (serving and advising clients) is the realm of the technician and is naturally the role that most planners fulfill in the early stages of their business. At some point, they recognize the need to hire an operational resource to take care of the manager dimension.

In order to mature and evolve, the firm must be able to add and retire services, reshape operational models, and pivot into new lines of business. These initiatives are the realm of the entrepreneur, whose vision should ultimately guide the firm.

Such visionary activities typically involve a new initiative, such as opening a new office. This may demand considerable time and resources in the immediate term and deliver a return that may not materialize until long in the future.

As Gerber outlines, there is a natural tension between the entrepreneur's need to disrupt and the manager's need to conserve. This tension is highest at the point where the vision clashes with the needs of the present day. The best way to resolve this tension peacefully is to base the discussion in data.

> "The hourly firm understands its starting point with respect to time and resources, with the exactness that only accurate data can provide."

The hourly firm understands its starting point with respect to time and resources, with the exactness that only accurate data can provide. It is thus uniquely in a position to have this grounded discussion.

The long-term vision, furthermore, can be deconstructed into concrete steps and requirements of time and resources set against these steps to assess whether they are achievable and at what expense to the current business.

Working with a common dataset, the entrepreneur and manager, who need each other to survive, can realize their combined potential.

The benefits of the hourly model can be summed up in two words: *clarity* and *control*.

- Clarity for the client ensures that the exchange of fees for value is fair and seen to be fair.
- Control for the business owner enables the firm to operate efficiently and yet remain agile.

As well as bringing benefits, the unique aspects of the hourly model bring their own set of challenges, which we will discuss in the next chapter.

Chapter 3

Mountains (& Molehills)

Although hourly is not a new system, its application to financial planning is still relatively recent, and, as such, it is possible to make a large number of mistakes in implementing it.

While the majority of this book is about how to do things right, in this chapter we focus on what to avoid.

Common Missteps

We start with common and easily avoidable missteps made by hourly planning firm owners:

- **Hedging on the fee model**: Instead of doing hourly on the side, you need to have a "burn the ships" mentality.
- **Going in cheap**: Clients link visual cues to the quality of your advice. Cutting corners on office decor and appearance is to be avoided.
- **Taking a project-based approach**: As covered earlier in the book, the aim should be to build relationships, not churn out plans.

- **Not tracking your time**: Predictably, this results in needless inefficiency and/or lost revenues.

Let's go through each of these in some more detail.

Hedging on the Fee Model

Charging by the hour exposes you: what you have done and what you have charged for is all there, itemized on the billing statement. This exposure is nothing to be afraid of and can work as a benefit.

Unfortunately, myths such as "Clients won't accept the fees" or "You can't make real money with this model" often remain, specter-like, in the minds of financial advisors contemplating the hourly approach, and even among hourly practitioners themselves.

This fear naturally creates a desire to hedge one's bets with these options: "Why go all-in on a model that will probably only work for some of the people some of the time?" or "Instead of putting all my eggs in one basket, I'll offer hourly as an option, but give my clients the freedom to choose."

This sounds like a really good idea. Different clients may be attracted to different fee models, and, therefore, advisors should reflect this in the way they charge. But, in practice, trying to run hourly in parallel with other fee models is a risky affair. To offer an analogy, it's like setting up a dance studio that teaches ballet and breakdancing and also doubles as a sushi bar.

In theory, this should maximize revenues by appealing to multiple segments. And while the customers definitely exist for these goods and services, the proprietor is unlikely to excel in serving them.

Similarly, running an hourly firm requires you to orient the entire business in a specific way, which we will cover in subsequent chapters. Alternating between fee models will militate against this, making an already difficult task all but impossible.

Going in Cheap

People are prepared to pay for value. But in the case of humans, as opposed to machines, value is as much to do with perception as it is rational calculation. Demonstrable expertise is a must, but unfortunately you cannot get by on expertise alone.

In other words, the service has to *feel* valuable as well as *be* valuable. Clients may not understand your area of expertise (that's why they're hiring you), so in order to be reassured that you are an expert, they will be looking for visual and tangible cues.

Some hourly planners believe their business is inherently a high-volume, low-margin proposition. They assume, therefore, that they should keep costs low by dressing down, going virtual, and adopting a no-frills approach.

> "Lower fees will potentially decrease your client's willingness to follow your advice."

There's nothing inherently wrong with any of these practices. But together they will create a low-budget ambience and impact your ability to charge your worth. Lower fees means lower profitability, but just as importantly, they will potentially decrease your client's willingness to follow your advice.

Everyone likes a bargain, but only in certain contexts. How much trust would you put in a cheap life vest, a cut-price dentist, or a rock-bottom wedding planning service, staffed with indifferent college students on a minimum wage?

The conversations you have with your clients are no less impactful than the conversations they will be having with other professional advisors. Dressing formally and adopting the demeanor and external accoutrements of other professions, though costly, is an important part of your value and right to charge.

Taking a Project-based Approach

This follows on from the idea that hourly is transactional rather than relational. As we have stressed, a strong client relationship is neither created nor negated by the fee model, but is a result of the advisor's own attitude.

This means that a planner who approaches the job as a series of transactions is inevitably destined to build a project-centric business. They will spend most of their time trying to acquire new clients when they could be serving existing ones.

The initial financial plan is only a part—and a small one at that—of the rich and broad category of activities that is financial *planning*. Unfortunately, the two (plan and planning) are often confused because they sound almost identical.

> "The default assumption should be that clients are looking for an ongoing relationship, unless they state otherwise."

It is unsurprising that if we present clients with a narrow view of planning, they will accept it and exit the office holding the plan thinking the job is done.

A planner who sees their role as a guide through the perpetually changing landscape of life will convey this view naturally to their clients through the advice process, and follow-on meetings will arise as a logical consequence of the ongoing process.

Since an ongoing relationship is where the bulk of the value of having an advisor lies, the default assumption should be that clients are looking for an ongoing relationship, unless they state otherwise.

Not Tracking Your Time

Tracking your time is vital because it ensures the following:

- You are charging accurately.
- You can explain the price to clients.
- You can make a reasonable profit from your work.

These points seem obvious. So why make them?

Some hourly planners don't track their time because it is easier not to. But this shortcut comes at a longer-term commercial cost.

To avoid the risk of overestimating the time spent on billable work, and potentially overcharging their clients, such planners may deliberately underestimate the bill to be on the safe side. Noble as this may seem, by effectively discounting their fees without even being asked to, they are damaging their ability to grow and even serve their existing clients effectively.

In other words, this is not noble but lazy. It is also dangerous. Even if the business does grow, different planners will have different approaches to estimating. Since there can be no formalized way of deliberately underestimating the bill, the result will be a mess, in the worst scenario verging on the unethical.

Time-tracking, as we have stated elsewhere, is not only highly achievable, but repays the additional modest effort it requires many times over.

The Next Level

The previous points explain common but avoidable errors. Overcoming them should be considered a basic requirement for running a successful hourly firm.

In addition to these molehills, there are genuine mountains to climb. To prepare yourself for the climb, we are providing a list of the main obstacles you will face along the way. We include a brief explanation and solution for each hurdle and will dive deeper in later chapters.

As with the benefits in chapter 2, these bigger challenges are divided into client-facing and internal issues.

Client-facing Challenges

Challenge 1: Needing to "sell" the model to people unfamiliar with it.

This challenge is not a continuous one. Most clients who come to you will be looking for an hourly planning relationship and are already sold on the model. But because most people are familiar with other ways of delivering and charging for financial advice, there may be initial bewilderment. This is particularly the case among centers of influence or COIs—oddly enough, as they themselves typically charge by the hour. (COIs are adjacent professionals such as lawyers and accountants who are in a position to refer their clients to financial advisors for financial questions.)

Pushback may take the form of apprehension ("You're asking me to write a blank check?") or genuine incomprehension ("What do you mean you don't manage my money?"). They may even request another fee model ("How about a flat fee?").

The issue will probably be raised toward the end of the meeting, when clients are expecting a firm, ongoing commitment on yearly fees or a cap, and realize that, in general, the fee cannot be known for certain in advance.

> "Over time, clients typically develop an intuitive grasp of the time-value relationship."

Solution: As we will cover later in the book, hourly does not mean playing it by ear. By the end of the first meeting, a planner should have a fairly good idea of the final fee for the *initial* planning engagement and should communicate this to the client. It is harder, if not impossible, to project further out into the future, beyond the initial planning and onboarding phase.

Over time, clients typically develop an intuitive grasp of the time-value relationship. In Mark's experience, different folks can take different amounts of time to develop this intuition or fine-tuning.

While this is taking place, working with ranges can be a helpful way to set expectations.

The key for the planner is not to be held hostage by this challenge. As we are in danger of repeating *ad infinitum*: your commercial terms as an hourly planner are the same as those of the other hourly professionals who serve your clients.

Challenge 2: You need to show value for every dime.

The majority of planners work extremely hard, but there are zero hourly planners who do not. In this respect, the hourly model is quite unforgiving. Skeptics worry that the hourly model will give the impression to clients that they are being nickel-and-dimed for every service.

The experience of working on an hourly basis, where every penny must be earned, is akin to this feeling, but in reverse. This relentless link between work and compensation is a large part of why the hourly model is attractive for clients—and often cheaper than the alternatives.

Furthermore, for the advisor, an afternoon's golf comes at the expense of an afternoon's earnings and requires a conscious commercial decision to trade revenue for a work-free afternoon.

Solution: Hard work is a fact of life for most professionals. It is a sign that you are adding value, and (for hourly planners) that you are earning money.

The biggest problem is *not* having enough work, which is only likely to be an issue in the early years of an hourly firm, as is the case for any start-up. You can offset this risk by entering the process with enough capital to fund the initial section of the growth curve (although this process does not need to be lengthy; see chapter 7 for more detail).

Unlike other firms, the disparity between market supply (currently miniscule) and market demand (enormous) should ensure that work soon picks up. The KPI to look out for is the proportion of initial work versus recurring work. A firm that has reached steady-state growth following the initial start-up period should aim for a split of 25% initial to 75% ongoing.

Challenge 3: Transparency on fees can trigger challenges on price.

There's no doubt that the hourly model raises awareness that there is an exchange of money for value taking place. The saliency of the hourly fee is by no means a showstopper, but it is the point around which price negotiations will typically revolve.

Occasionally, therefore, it is to be expected that clients will question the bill or seek a discount.

Solution: The future success of your business rests in large part on your ability to defend your price model during these moments, rare though they may be. There is no single correct response to a price challenge; the method used depends on the individual. Appeals to reason might work in one scenario; whereas, another might require psychological reframing (for example, calculate the equivalent in basis points).

"If the client is not a good fit for the model, you are both better off finding this out sooner rather than later."

There are ways to decrease the price if a client is willing to work with a more junior advisor, and if their situation warrants. It is also possible to spread the bill out over time if they are temporarily unable to pay. We'll address the topic of pricing negotiation in more detail in chapter 6.

The fundamental rule is this: Be steadfast on hourly rates. There is rarely a good reason to charge less than you are worth, except in industries with overcapacity issues. This is not the case with financial planning.

Furthermore, as an hourly planner, discounting fees is one of the most damaging actions that you can do to your value proposition, let alone your bottom line. If a relationship founders on pricing, it is a sign that the client is not a good fit for the model, and you are both better off finding this out sooner rather than later.

Internal Challenges

Challenge 4: The need for processes.

In Challenge 1, we pointed out the unyielding equation nested within the hourly fee model: No work = No fees. The equivalent on the operational side is: No process = No profit.

In an hourly firm, inefficiency is felt keenly, either by the business itself (higher costs lead to lower profits) or by the client (higher fees to maintain profit margins).

Irrespective of whether the advisor decides that lower profits are acceptable, an inefficient business will sooner or later be perceived as such by the client, and this may lead them to wonder if *they* are the ones who are paying the cost.

Solution: The best approach to solving the problem of accurate billing and efficient management is comprehensive time-tracking. Timesheet data provides a high-resolution view of the status quo, and is the basis for an informed discussion about how processes can be re-designed or replaced.

When the underlying problem or process is addressed, time-tracking data will also confirm if and to what extent the problem has been fixed. See chapters 8 and 9 for more details on what this looks like.

Challenge 5: People management.

Processes and tools are needed to ensure that time is managed effectively. But the other key element of value—expertise—is dependent on the people who carry out these processes.

With no products or investment returns to hide behind, the people of an hourly firm are not the greatest asset it possesses, they are the *only* asset. And, of course, people can also be a liability if they are not a cultural fit, do not adapt to the processes required to make the hourly firm work, or simply do not perform.

As with processes, problems arising from people issues will quickly show up in the financials of the firm through dissatisfied clients disputing bills, requesting to switch advisors, or simply leaving after the third administrative snafu this quarter.

Solution: If an hourly firm is to grow beyond a solo practice, the founder must commit to becoming an excellent people manager (or to hiring one). This is not a commitment that many solo practitioners will want to make.

If so, fair enough. The best strategy for such advisors is to remain a solo practitioner and focus on high-complexity clients (that is, maximal revenue per head --> fewer clients overall --> less time needed for administration).

> "The people of an hourly firm are not the greatest asset it possesses, they are the *only* asset."

But an owner who wants to expand the reach of the firm to impact more lives must accept that this goal is incompatible with a willingness to subsidize ineffectual but well-meaning employees. Even if you are prepared to fund a charity, the clients of the firm should not be asked to contribute.

Challenge 6: Planning is nonnegotiable.

The ability to offer financial advice to a wider range of clients at a lower average price than the competition comes at the cost of constant vigilance by the owner or firm head. This vigilance must not only be focused on the day-to-day issues of process and people management, but must also be forward-looking, as the challenges of an hourly business morph as the firm grows.

Hiring new advisors, for instance, creates new capacity (approximately 1,200 hours each, assuming 60% utilization). But these resources will earn only to the extent that they are utilized, and training them will eat into the earning and prospecting hours of the main advisor.

After the advisors are trained and begin to mature, the question of partnership comes into focus, bringing with it the benefits of shared risk and more leadership input, as well as the dilution of control and the potential for discord over the firm's future.

Solution: To be dealt with, the above problems have to be seen in advance, as they are generally too big to react to when they have already begun to cause problems (and problems in an hourly firm typically have an immediate financial impact, owing to the 1:1 ratio of activities to revenue).

In the benefits chapter, we observed that the hourly planning firm, with superior data and control levers, has a unique ability to plan its future. We should add that this ability to plan brings with it a necessity to plan, if this future is to be bright.

Just as the business will not run itself, the business will not scale itself either, and the owner must constantly reappraise the status quo and plan for the next turn in the road. We cover this in more detail in chapter 9.

In setting out the challenges discussed in this chapter, we wanted to provide a different perspective to the previous chapters, which tended to focus on the positives of going hourly.

As we have shown, none of the benefits of the hourly model come for free. Facing these challenges requires competence and determination. If you have the potential to complete this journey, you are most likely motivated rather than discouraged at this point. So let's move to the next level of detail.

PART 2

SERVING
THE CLIENT

Chapter 4

Offering: "So, what do you do?"

The benefits of planning are typically described generically, as if planning were a one-size-fits-all proposition. This generic description is better than nothing, especially for someone who has zero knowledge of the field. But it is rather like a lawyer who says, "We help you win cases." Accurate as far as it goes, but inadequate.

Like lawyers, financial planners deal with a wide range of client problems, and there are almost infinite variations of the planning support they can offer.

How the Hourly Mindset Helps

One might think that an hourly practice has the least coherent offering of all. Since you are just charging for time, there is no "offering"—you are simply reacting to client needs.

In fact, the reverse is true.

While many planners may have a sense that some clients are more work than others, the hourly planner can describe with precision how clients differ, both quantitatively and qualitatively. Self-evidently, a client who is billed for ten hours in a given year has received a quantitatively different service than the client who is billed for 100 hours.

Delving into the detail behind these two offerings, the hourly planner can, if requested, qualitatively deconstruct each into its constituent parts. This high-resolution view allows advisors to think in more granular and systematic terms about different client types, needs, and services (see Figure 1).

Client Situation	Client Complexity	Advice Needed
• Divorcing • Recently bereaved • Inheritance • Seeking validation	• # of individuals involved (such as family) • Nature of wealth (fragmented, for example)	• Cash flow/retirement plan • Investment advice • Risk management • Estate planning

Figure 1: From needs to service.

With a clear vision of what needs to be done for each client (or prospective client) based on their situation, an advisor can better plan their work and be proactive in helping the client through the process.

"No matter how clear a picture an advisor forms, the future will always deviate from expectations."

Needless to say, no matter how clear a picture an advisor forms of a given client's future needs, the future will always deviate from expectations in one way or another (see Figure 2). Part of what is delivered can be planned, and the remainder must be tailored to circumstance.

Time

Unpredictability

Predictability

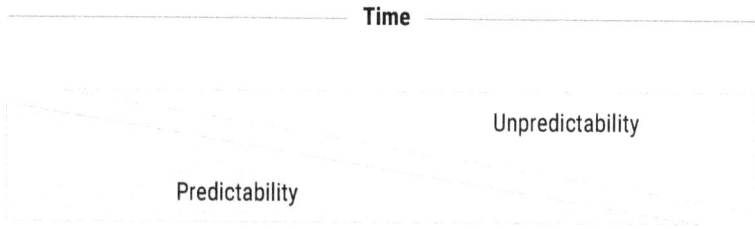

Figure 2: Needs are less easy to predict with time.

A Broader Canvas

When deciding which clients to serve, the hourly planner has much greater freedom than the typical advisor. The typical advisor is confined to targeting clients with a minimum amount of liquid wealth (high net worth individuals) or those about to come into it (such as pre-retirees, business owners approaching a sale).

The hourly advisor can, of course, serve these clients, but it is also possible, and perhaps preferable, to target the "blue ocean" that remains inaccessible to most financial advisors. This ocean is vast: since everyone can benefit from financial advice, the addressable market excludes only those who absolutely lack the ability to pay.

The traditional "high net worth delegator" market, which accounts for around 1 to 2% of the population, still represents a fraction of the market reachable by the hourly model.

Helping People Earlier

By the time an individual reaches fifty-five, many of the most important financial decisions have already been made (and possibly fumbled). It is at this point that most financial advisors arrive on the scene, targeting those who have been wise or fortunate enough to manage the most difficult part of the journey alone.

The hourly advisor can happily stray from the familiar pre-retiree (ages fifty-five to sixty-five) hunting ground and help clients earlier in their lives. In advising clients in their twenties and thirties, the hourly planner is helping to create more wealthy pre-retirees in the future.

Let's say that only one in five reach this pre-retirement point successfully without an advisor. By targeting the other four before they make critical mistakes, it could be possible to double or triple the future high net worth market.

Helping DIY Clients

As well as thinking vertically in terms of different age groups, it is also possible to think horizontally within them.

Even among the high net worth segment, not all wealth is liquid, and not all those who have liquid wealth like the idea of paying someone to take charge of it, especially in an age of cheap investment management.

(There is a common misconception that hourly clients are invariably DIY or do-it-yourself investors. In our experience, they are as likely to be validators who want advice on their investments but not full-blown management and are hence left homeless within the prevailing system.)

The hourly model, therefore, addresses the planning needs of two new groups (see Figure 3): the unserved (younger clients) and the underserved (nondelegator wealthy clients).

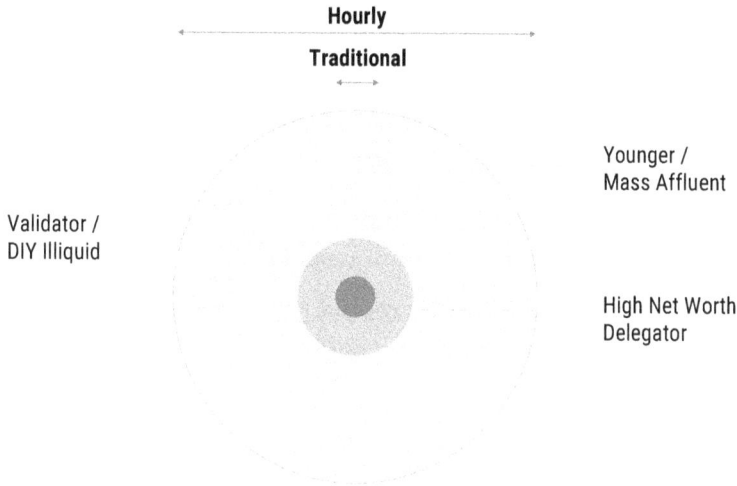

Figure 3: Why be satisfied with the bull's-eye when you can have the entire target?

Segmentation and Niches

One definition of a niche is that you will turn away a prospect who falls outside your target group to make room for a client who falls within it. The reasons for doing this are marketing and efficiency:

- **Marketing:** It differentiates you from other advisors. Your target client will choose you because you serve people like them.
- **Efficiency:** You will work better and faster because you know your client's problems and have dealt with them before.

The most familiar way of segmenting clients is by the amount of wealth they have to invest. This is important for planners who price based on assets under management (AUM), but is irrelevant for an hourly planner.

Occupation-based niches (such as dentists, or executives at large corporations with complex retirement/compensation arrangements) are increasingly common as well and bring both of the advantages above (marketing and efficiency) to the traditional advisor who builds a firm around them.

For an hourly advisor, however, niches are not so important. Why? Let's go back to the two points just expressed:

- **Marketing:** The hourly model is so rare that it is in and of itself a differentiator—and an unusual one.
- **Efficiency:** The hourly model is naturally efficient, because it has to be. The last three chapters of this book explain this in more detail.

Because the hourly practice can serve anybody, regardless of wealth level, and remain profitable, regardless of the size of the problem or need, it is by default niche-agnostic.

The hourly advisor should have a target group, but for different reasons. The ideal client profile is more likely to do with personality or compatibility factors (such as faith and values), which ensure the relationship will be pleasant and productive.

"Because the hourly practice can serve anybody, it is by default niche-agnostic."

This last point is not a trivial one. It may be a saving grace of the hourly model that all time, however stressful, is at least compensated. But if you take whoever walks through the door, the odds are that you will end up with a sprinkling of dysfunctional relationships that disproportionately sap your energy and so impact your ability to serve everyone else.

Conversely, working with clients whose company you enjoy means less needless stress for the advisor and higher receptiveness on the part of the client. Long term, being selective is the best way to grow your business.

Identifying Client Needs

Once you have identified the criteria that describe your target client group, you must then consider their needs. Broadly, two elements determine the nature and quantity of advice needed: situation and complexity.

- **Situation** dictates the type of issues a client will need advice on.
- **Complexity** (= moving parts involved) determines the amount of time required.

Life Situations

An hourly planner will end up speaking to clients from a wide variety of situations besides the wealthy pre-retiree category. It is vital to pay attention to where your client is starting from in order to form an accurate picture of their needs.

You should encourage your advisors (and yourself) to keep asking the question for every new prospect: "What is the reason this person wants to hire us?"

> "While life stages are a rough-and-ready guide to how needs progress over time, an advisor deals with individuals and not averages."

It is easy to fall back on pre-made answers and tactical solutions rather than get to the heart of the client's needs. While life stages are a rough-and-ready guide to how needs progress over time, an advisor deals with individuals and not averages (see Figure 4).

Bad experience investing my own money	We're thinking of buying a house	Received an inheritance, overwhelmed
Doctor Late 30s	**Professional couple** Late 20s	**Homemaker** Early 50s
Have not thought through succession / sale	Unsure if I can financially support daughter	Finances are complex, not sure what I'm doing
Business owner Early 50s	**Post-retiree** Early 70s	**Executive** Late 30s

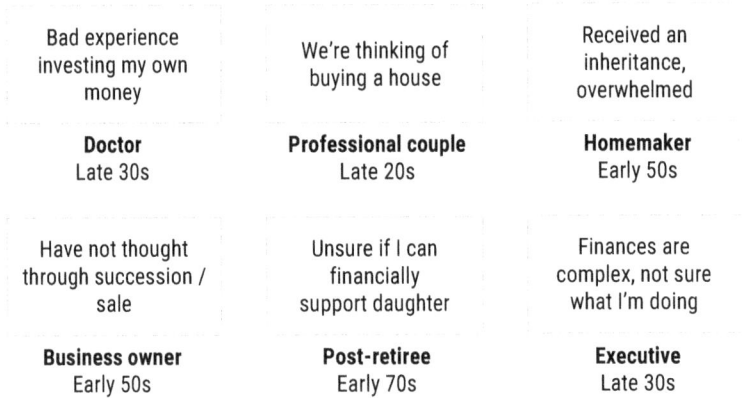

Figure 4: Starting situations are all slightly different.

Drivers of Complexity

Complexity is a question of moving parts and can vary considerably among clients in the same situation. Complexity is the dimension that will ultimately determine the quantity of time and effort (hence fees) for an individual client.

As already stated, the individual case is what is important, and not the typical case. People in ostensibly the same situation and life stage can vary considerably in their complexity. This is why in Mark's business, complexity is the primary lever of segmentation. It is measured using a system of levels from 1 to 5, with level 5 the most complex.

Figure 5 displays how the effort required by clients at different levels of complexity can vary in the first year, when the initial plan is being prepared.

Complexity	Effort to deliver (hours) 1st year: initial financial plan
Level 5	40+
Level 4	25-40
Level 3	15-30
Level 2	12-25
Level 1	10-20

Figure 5: Effort and variability increase with complexity.

Common, more straightforward needs such as how to manage cash flow are covered in levels 1–2. Less common, more time-intensive issues, such as deferred compensation, are addressed in levels 3–5.

More complexity does not necessarily mean more time with the client, but will almost certainly mean more preparation time. Meeting preparation can last from forty-five minutes to twenty hours depending on the level of complexity.

Various complexity schedules provide a guide to what is involved at each level in various areas of planning. Here is the complexity schedule for Estate Planning Counsel/Design.

Estate Services	Complexity levels				
	1	2	3	4	5
Basic estate planning advice	☑	☑	☑	☑	☑
Estate design	☑	☑	☑	☑	☑
Review of existing documents		☑	☑	☑	☑
Charitable estate planning			☑	☑	☑
Estate settlement advice				☑	☑
Irrevocable trusts					☑

The lowest level addresses fundamental needs. Additional elements of complexity (preexisting plans, philanthropy, and so on) creep in as the level rises. This complexity lens gives clarity to both client and advisor. It also creates a shorthand for discussions with centers of influence about potential referrals.

> "This complexity lens creates a shorthand for discussions with centers of influence about potential referrals."

If a CPA knows the target client profile for an individual advisor, they are more likely to make a confident referral upon seeing a client who corresponds to it. The following example illustrates the point.

A CPA once said to Mark, "Most planning firms want to work with a level 5 client just before the liquidity event."

Mark replied, "Where we see the need is ten years before. If we do the pre-work, and get the framework in place, we can avoid a rush of uncoordinated decisions."

The CPA happened to know someone who was about ten years away from just such an event and promptly made the referral.

A final point on level 5 clients: While it is possible to assign levels 1-4 to fairly well-defined ranges of complexity, level 5 is unique in that it theoretically has no ceiling. When one discusses level 5 clients, one is talking about a client that has surpassed a certain threshold, rather than a recognizable "type".

Matching Resources to Needs

Dealing with levels of complexity makes it easier to assign appropriately experienced resources.

At Timothy Financial, there are four advisor career stages:

- **Lead Advisor:** Manages engagements for the most complex clients (level 5) in addition to mentoring and firm marketing activities.

- **Senior Advisor:** Primarily client-facing, with exposure to more complex clients (levels 3–4). Also involved in firm marketing and prospecting.

- **Financial Advisor:** Serves basic clients (levels 1–2) in a client-facing capacity, but mainly supports senior and lead advisors in serving more complex clients.

- **Financial Planner:** Not client-facing, but supports in a paraplanner capacity, across all complexity levels.

Note: At Timothy Financial, these descriptions are not set in stone. An advisor can choose to remain at a complexity level (say level 2 or 3) while mentoring, marketing, and prospecting.

Particularly in complex cases, clients will be served by teams rather than individual advisors. The mix of expertise will be geared toward the advisor with the most appropriate skillset.

Nonsystematic Variability

As set out above, life stage gives a general sense of the needs of a client at a given point in time, and complexity levels make it possible to home in on the specifics of a given client situation. As also noted, no matter how much an advisor understands about the client, the future remains unpredictable.

There are two factors that contribute to this nonsystematic category of needs: happenstance and client preference.

Happenstance

"The best laid plans of mice and men," so the saying goes. Inheritance windfalls, changes in marital status, bereavements, new arrivals, kids moving out, elderly parents moving in. None of these events happen according to a spreadsheet.

Mark had a meeting with a client who told him in the first few seconds of the discussion that he had stage 4 colon cancer. In an instant, the preparation for the meeting was out the window, and the nature of the work changed materially.

It is never possible to tell what clients will do or what will happen to them, nor the effect that these life changes will have on their financial lives or the meticulous plans and projections of last quarter. This is why a true financial planning engagement is never an event or transaction, but rather an ongoing process of adaptation to the twists and turns of life.

Client Preference

The advisor may be navigating, but the client is in the driver's seat. The nature and the extent of the service delivered is ultimately within their power.

That is why client preference is the second nonsystematic factor that determines what the advisor ultimately delivers and charges for. As an hourly planner, you need to accommodate, so far as possible, the wishes of the client in addition to your own counsel.

Client preferences can go in one of two directions: asking for less and asking for more.

Asking for Less

The first case is trickiest and typically presents itself in the form of the client lite. This client believes that it is possible to extract the value of advice without having to pay for what they would call the padding: "Don't worry about making a plan, just tell me what I should do."

The planner in this situation is like a doctor being asked to provide the results of an MRI scan without conducting the scan itself.

In such cases, it is best to tactfully explain why a full planning relationship is necessary to provide an answer to the client's questions. If the client is unwilling to comprehend the message, the meeting (and relationship) is likely over.

Asking for More

The most straightforward example would be a client who asks the advisor to help a family member or facilitate a family meeting. Family-related work is one of the main factors that contributes to variability of workload from client to client, year to year.

But the more that a client is asking for may go outside the realm of the purely financial, pertaining to the psychological or irrational dimensions of money. This may well still be in the advisor's purview.

Mark has two long-standing clients, a husband and wife, who have a vast fortune and whose dependents are taken care of. Theoretically, they have no need that they are fulfilling, but the ongoing reassurance they receive from their yearly meetings is psychologically important for them.

It is common for level 5 clients (such as senior executives, business owners) to seek a financial advisor as a form of psychological refuge from being the decision-maker whom everyone consults, but who has no one else to go to for advice.

There is also the case of a disorganized client who may require more hand-holding and support. The hourly model creates a means of compensating the advisor for the additional effort, as well as an incentive for the client to improve.

There are, however, boundaries that you should draw. Clients who bring full-blown psycho-therapeutic issues to the meeting should be helped to find other professionals better suited to support them.

Drawing the threads together (see Figure 6), we can see that (outside of a very narrow range of cases) we simply cannot predict what a client will need.

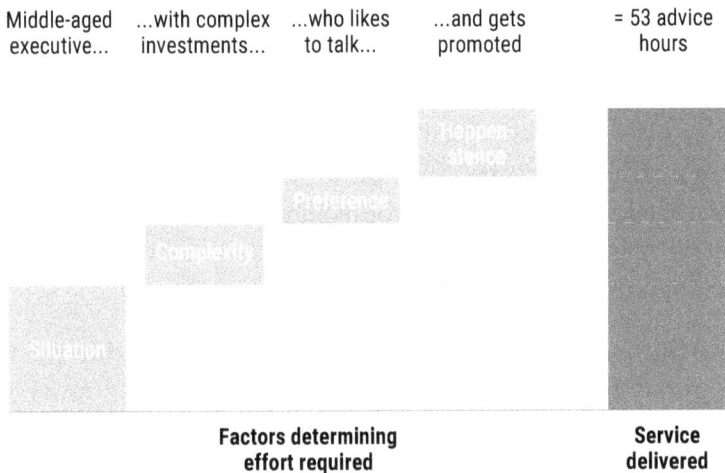

Figure 6: The final deliverable is the product of multiple forces.

Should I advise on investments as well as financial planning?

It may occur to an hourly advisor to ask whether they would be better off doing planning only and leaving investment advice to others. In our opinion, you cannot be a comprehensive planner *without* advising on investments.

Investment advice is not the same as managing money. In other words, you do not have custody but you can, for instance, offer advice on opportunities for tax-loss harvesting, asset allocation and investment selection, or help a client to negotiate asset management fees with a third party.

An hourly planner is able to divest the costly paraphernalia of the professional money manager (portfolio management software), saving time and expense without any real loss of value to the client. This also gives the advisor freedom to advise on any type of investment or product. Whether assets are "held-away" or with multiple custodians, there is no transfer or re-papering required.

> "Viewed properly, investments and planning are inseparable."

Just as investments cannot be excluded, we would also counsel against giving investment advice *outside* the context of planning. Viewed properly, investments and planning are inseparable.

In summary, the hourly planner's offering is rich and clearly defined but requires all the more skill to deliver and to discern what to give to whom and when. Having a purposeful approach to classifying clients by need allows the planner to match clients with resources of appropriate skill. Proactivity on the part of these advisors ensures that changing client needs are identified and addressed in time.

Chapter 5

Pricing: Handle with Care

In the last chapter, we traced a path from the client's needs to the offering provided by the firm. To reiterate, this offering is a function of two elements:

- **Time**: meetings, preparation, and follow-up
- **Expertise**: appropriate resource(s) for the tasks

If you multiply total hours (= time) by an appropriate hourly rate (= expertise), you have the final bill. If calculating the bill is as simple as this, why do we need an entire chapter on pricing?

The Central Role of Pricing

Pricing is important because it creates revenue, which pays for everything. As an hourly planner, when you run out of hours, you run out of the ability to earn. Since monetizing the hours you have is the only path to revenue, an hourly business will flourish or flounder according to how well the hourly rate is set and enforced.

> "Pricing is important because it creates revenue, which pays for everything."

Pricing is never simple, because it is ultimately tied to human psychology.

We are referring here not only to the psychology of the client, but also to that of the advisor. Nine times out of ten, the main enemy in the struggle to charge for value is likely to be the latter and not the former.

This is particularly likely to be the case with hourly planners, who have historically (for whatever reason) been prone to underprice, undercharge, and hence underachieve. An hourly firm that gets pricing wrong will fail to grow and so deprive many potential clients of advice, and many planners of potential employment.

> "Hourly planners have historically (for whatever reason) been prone to underprice, undercharge, and hence underachieve."

The purpose of this chapter is to demonstrate how to avoid this fate. As always, pricing policies and approaches that are quite feasible in traditional firms must be reexamined and, if necessary, replaced.

Back to Basics

In the opening chapter on myths, we briefly touched on the misconception that hourly pricing is a cost-based approach. Cost-plus pricing (estimated cost per hour + % margin) is a suboptimal pricing methodology for a number of reasons, chiefly because it fails to reflect willingness to pay or, in other words, value to the client.

It also often fails to achieve the one goal it sets out to accomplish, which is to ensure profitability. Since you can never truly predict revenues, in the presence of fixed costs you can never be sure that the planned profit margin will materialize.

Charging for time and expertise, on the other hand, is the purest way to link fees paid to value delivered—hence, we would argue, is the purest form of value-based pricing for financial planning.

It is common to hear the objection, "But what about the time we save our clients? What about the tax savings? What about peace of mind? What about the goals we help bring to life?"

To be sure, the benefits of financial planning extend in many directions, and an experienced advisor can have a substantial impact on a client's life in a relatively short period of time. **It seems fair to ask why planners should not charge based on the impact (results achieved) rather than on the input (time and expertise).**

Impact-based Pricing

If you want to charge based on results, you have to be able to quantify those results down to the dollar.

Because the benefits of financial advice spill over into so many areas of a client's life, both financial and nonfinancial, they are notoriously hard to quantify in this way. No one has so far been able to do so with precision.

But even if it were possible to charge based on the results of financial advice, with no difficulties in quantification or disputes over responsibility, we would maintain that it is not consistent with the concept of professional advice to do so.

Would you consider a doctor who performed a life-saving operation to have some kind of ongoing claim on the life of the patient? Should a tennis coach automatically claim a share of the prize money?

Just as the patient might not survive without the efforts of the surgeon, or the tennis player might lose the championship without the efforts of the coach, many clients would forfeit millions without the timely intervention of a financial planner, but the doctor, the tennis coach, and the advisor are ultimately service providers.

When the patient leaves the operating room, the tennis champion steps out on the court, and the client leaves the advisor's office, whatever benefits accrue from then on are theirs to keep (or to lose). None of which means that you can't charge based on value.

An hourly planner who feels their advice is worth $10,000 per hour is free to charge this rate, and clients who perceive the value will pay for it.

Setting Levels by Resource

So how does one decide on the hourly rate?

In the case of law, expertise is clearly a driver, with partners billing higher rates than associates. Rates also vary widely by field (for example, civil litigation vs. criminal defense). Thus it is possible for an associate at one firm to be billed out at a higher rate than a partner working for another firm.

We suspect that the ultimate driver behind hourly rates is complexity. Some fields are more complex than others, and within a given field, experience (= expertise) is required to approach more complex cases.

In the case of Timothy Financial, this complexity is captured in the levels 1–5, introduced earlier, with more complex clients requiring not only more time but also more expertise and therefore a higher hourly rate (see Figure 7).

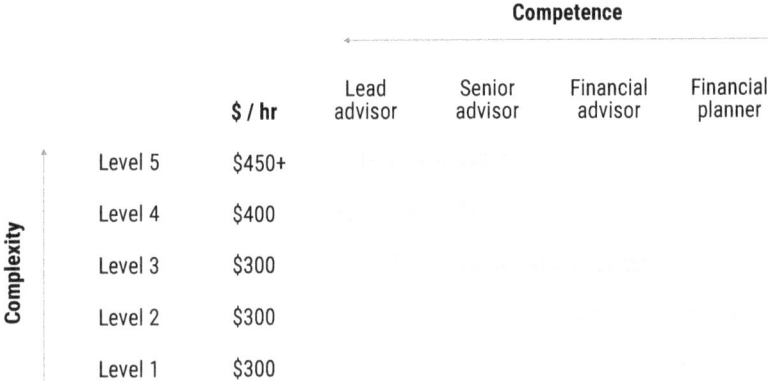

		Competence			
	$ / hr	Lead advisor	Senior advisor	Financial advisor	Financial planner
Level 5	$450+				
Level 4	$400				
Level 3	$300				
Level 2	$300				
Level 1	$300				

(Complexity increases from Level 1 to Level 5, shown on vertical axis)

Figure 7: Higher Complexity = Higher Competence = Higher Hourly Rate.

You will see that for level 5, the quoted hourly rate has a "+" sign next to it. As already mentioned in chapter 4, level 5 has no ceiling to the complexity it can contain. While $450 per hour may be applicable for many or most level 5 clients, those of extraordinarily high complexity may require a different advisor, and hence a different rate.

In the case of Timothy Financial, this advisor is Mark, who charges his clients $600 per hour, as of the time of writing.

Calculating Rates

Where do these rates come from? It is not, as we have said before, a case of cost plus target margin.

For any goods or services, the process of price discovery relies on an accurate understanding of

- **Willingness to pay**: whether the client views the price as fair, and
- **Ability to pay**: whether the price is within the client's means.

Willingness to pay will increase in proportion to an advisor's experience and ability and is the primary driver behind the hourly firm's rates for its senior advisors.

Ability to pay will be the driving factor behind the lower rates, in the case of younger clients for whom junior advisors are both a more affordable and appropriate fit.

Setting a Ceiling

Setting and enforcing higher rates for senior advisors is crucial. This rate allows the firm to monetize the hard-won expertise of their most experienced advisors. But it also serves as an indicator of quality to the clients whom they serve.

Even for clients who pay the lower rates, the upper rates create a reference point that puts their fees in context. So, $300 per hour might seem expensive in isolation, but quite reasonable when compared with $600 per hour.

Indeed, charging substantially higher rates for more experienced advisors ultimately enables the business to take on clients with a lower ability to pay. Charging everyone the same rate, by contrast, would exclude a significant portion of the potential base.

How high can you go on the hourly rate for the upper end of financial planning?

The going rate among senior planners has not been systematically documented but appears anecdotally to be in the range of $400 to $500 per hour. The law of supply and demand alone suggests that hourly planners in general could, if they wished to, charge higher rates than they do now, given the comparatively large number of clients that cannot be served by the prevailing model.

We see rates in excess of $1,000 per hour for leading attorneys. Arguably, the service provided by some financial planners is worth even more than this.

Managing Your Time

It is common for inquiring clients to ask to speak to the head of the firm. If the client is complex and requires maximal expertise, this request may make sense. More often, the request is an attempt by the client to ensure they get the best level of service.

"Higher rates serve as a natural regulator to ensure efficient channeling of time and resources."

The time of a senior planner, especially the founder, is precious, and spending it on lower-complexity or lower-paying work is damaging to the business.

When presented with a range of fees, the client may determine that they would be quite satisfied with an appropriate level of service—that is, a more junior resource at a lower hourly rate. Higher rates, therefore, serve as a natural regulator to ensure efficient channeling of time and resources.

Raising Rates

Finding the right fee is an ongoing process. As stated earlier, we think there is both room and rationale for hourly rates to go much higher for more experienced resources in the future. From a housekeeping perspective, it is necessary to raise rates periodically if only to keep up with inflation. Mark's approach is to raise fees by 10% every three years.

If the close rate is high (>80%) this is a sign that prices are not only acceptable but potentially too low, and therefore the increase in rates is both safe and justified. That said, pricing moves should always be handled with care.

There are psychological thresholds, particularly around natural boundary points (such as $100, $200, $300), where an increase can be processed as more salient. This is something to be aware of rather than constrained by.

Stopping just below the threshold (at, say, $295) is a way to postpone the effect, and when the boundary of $300 is crossed, it makes sense to do so wholeheartedly.

> "If handled properly, it is not unknown for close rates to actually increase when rates go up."

If handled properly, it is not unknown for close rates to actually increase when rates go up. Price is an indicator of value, and typical supply/demand dynamics do not apply when supply is constrained, as is the case with hourly financial planning.

It should be added that when a client is served by a team of advisors with differing hourly rates, the psychological thresholds of individual rates become less important.

Fixed Fees

The concept of a flat yearly fee is attractive because it provides certainty on revenues for the advisor and certainty on fees for the client. The problem is that planning needs are almost always uncertain.

The initial planning engagement is an exception that proves the rule. Onboarding a client and creating an initial plan is in many cases a standardized process, and variations in effort can be predicted with reasonable certainty based on past experience.

This is why clients of Timothy Financial receive a firm quote for the initial planning engagement during the first meeting. After the initial engagement, however, billing is 100% variable.

This may seem odd, as historical time-tracking data should in theory allow Mark and other hourly planners to predict with decent accuracy what future planning needs will likely arise for a client in a given situation.

Figures 8 and 9 display a selection of actual recorded hours for clients at various complexity levels. Could you have predicted them?

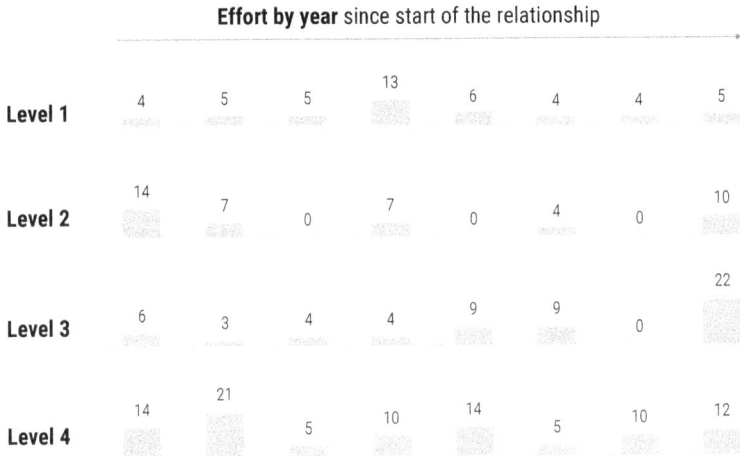

Effort by year since start of the relationship

Level 1	4	5	5	13	6	4	4	5
Level 2	14	7	0	7	0	4	0	10
Level 3	6	3	4	4	9	9	0	22
Level 4	14	21	5	10	14	5	10	12

Figure 8: Example clients for Levels 1 through 4 (number of hours).

Effort by year since start of the relationship

		141	114	138	162
Level 5 Client A	82				
Level 5 Client B	63	38	28	26	23
Level 5 Client C	4	29	56	70	78
Level 5 Client D	61	73	76	63	94

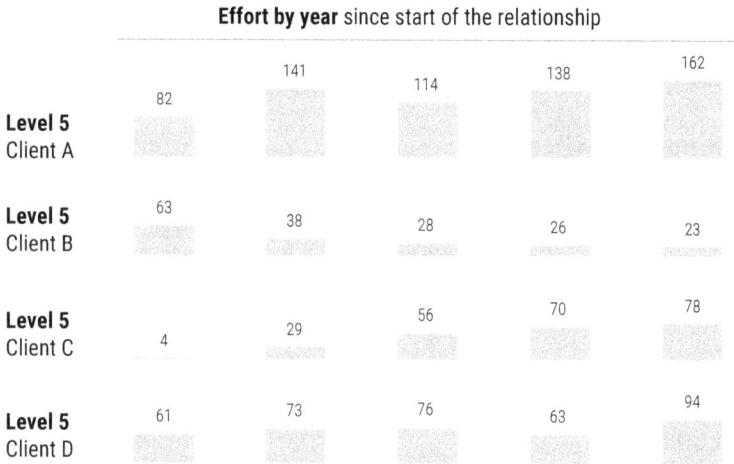

Figure 9: Example clients for Level 5 (number of hours).

As the data show, while it may be possible to accurately predict the average of a group, particularly in the case of the lower levels, for an individual it is virtually impossible.

Why is this?

One reason is that people with seemingly identical needs and backgrounds often have widely differing preferences, and these preferences often change over time. Clients A and B may be executives at the same stage of life and working for the same firm. But in an hourly relationship, one may opt to meet every other year, while the other requests the advisor to be present for every important meeting or phone call.

> "The hourly model can adapt perfectly without the need for prediction."

Furthermore, as a general rule, 5 to 10% of your clients will experience a major, unexpected life development in a given year. The nature of the unexpected is you don't know which ones it will happen to.

The hourly model can adapt perfectly to these twists and turns, without the need for prediction. Committing to a fixed fee, on the other hand, will result in either overcharging the client or undercompensating the business.

Mark inherited a client in his seventies who was used to paying his advisor a fixed yearly fee and requested to keep this arrangement. In the second year of the relationship, it emerged that one of the client's insurance policies was set to lapse in four years. The resulting work meant that more time was needed in year 2 than in year 1—an anomaly.

Aside from the unpredictability of client preferences and life events, there is a more fundamental reason why fixed fees are dangerous for financial planners, particularly in the case of a full-service firm with expertise in multiple domains (as opposed to more narrowly focused retirement planning).

In his book *Confessions of the Pricing Man: How Price Affects Everything*, Hermann Simon recalls a presentation he gave in the year 2000 to the mobile carrier T-Mobile, which was at that time under competitive pressure to offer more flat-rate subscriptions with unlimited data. He pointed out that a flat-rate system would result in a majority of light users subsidizing a small minority of heavy users, and this would lead with a high probability to lower revenue and profits.

As data usage grew in Europe, telecommunications companies were unable to monetize the additional user activity. Over a decade later, the CEO of Deutsche Telekom acknowledged that Professor Simon's predictions had been correct.

If the parallel between full-service financial planning and mobile data is apt, we should do well to heed the warning.

In both industries there is:

- A high incremental cost to additional usage—advice must be delivered by staff, who are expensive to train and retain; and

- A high potential for variability between users of similar complexity (preference and happenstance, as outlined above).

A fixed fee more or less guarantees that the hours delivered will most likely not equal the hours paid for. Someone is going to lose, and according to Simon's logic, it is likely to be the advisor. Conversely, the discipline that the hourly rate imposes—on both the advisor and client—is its beauty and its strength.

If we appear to belabor the point, it is only because the attraction of the fixed fee is so potent.

At the time we are writing this book, "fixed fee" is emerging as a standard alternative pricing tool for many advisors, typically as an accompaniment to the asset-based fee. It may well have a use as a floor mechanism in AUM-based pricing models, ensuring that clients do not fall below a certain revenue level.

But for an hourly practitioner offering comprehensive financial advice, the impreciseness of the fixed approach is fundamentally incompatible with the precision required to run the business itself.

Bulk Purchasing

There are ways to achieve a feeling of certainty without breaking the link between time and value.

The Fee Savings Scheme, which has been in use for two decades at Timothy Financial, is an example of this. Under the system, a client pre-purchases hours "in bulk" at a nominal discount. The money is held in a separate account, and fees for the actual hours incurred are deducted from this account until the balance is used up (unused balances are 100% refundable).

The client enjoys a small financial saving, but the main benefit is psychological. Dealing with multiple invoices, which can be trivial (such as a bill for seven minutes) is potentially annoying. The scheme converts fees into a series of predefined, periodic payments of equal size.

Installments

If a client is cash-constrained, or if a bill is particularly large, it may make sense to spread the bill over a longer period of time (possibly $100 per month until the bill is paid off). This arrangement is typically used only in exceptional cases involving real or perceived temporary financial hardship, rather than as a routine payment option.

As we began by asserting, the long-term success of any firm rests on its pricing. In the case of the hourly model, the chief concern should be to avoid the common tendency to undercharge, whether through lower rates or inaccurate estimates of time spent.

> "It is not the business that earns a profit that 'rips off' society. It is the business that fails to do so."

This does not mean that you will never lose money on a client, and, on some occasions, you may choose to do so. The important point is to avoid losing money becoming part of how you do business.

As we will see in the next chapter, your policy on discounts should be this: no discounts. We'll end with perhaps one of the greatest quotes on pricing ever spoken. It comes from an opinion piece in the *Wall Street Journal* in 1975, written by marketing expert Philip Kotler: "It is not the business that earns a profit adequate to its genuine costs of capital, to the risks of tomorrow and to the needs of tomorrow's worker and pensioner, that 'rips off' society. It is the business that fails to do so." If you don't charge your worth, you are not performing an act of charity, you are stealing from your employees and from your community. This runs counter to intuition, but is the reality of running a business.

Chapter 6

Communication: The Never-ending Story

While the ability to communicate the value of advice is important, for an hourly advisor, being a good salesperson is not. This may appear counterintuitive, because the hourly planner would appear at first glance to have the hardest sales job of all.

The pricing model focuses the client's attention entirely on the value of planning advice, as distinct from investment returns. As the client must hire the advisor for every meeting, the need to communicate this value is continuous. However, as discussed earlier, there are so many potential clients for whom hourly advice is the only option, and so few advisors offering it, the advisor very often has no competitors to "sell" against.

Even when there is competition—in the case of high net worth clients, for example—the hourly planner is in all likelihood offering similar or better value at a price point orders of magnitude lower than the closest alternative.

There are aspects of communicating the value of the offering that apply more or less uniquely to hourly planners, and these will be our focus in this chapter.

Marketing

Attracting suitable clients (and filtering out unsuitable ones) is straightforward for the hourly advisor. While many advisor websites look similar to one another, and seldom explain fees in any level of detail, the hourly planning firm can address both of these issues by positioning the fee model front and center.

Simply having the words *hourly planner* will propel you to the top of a search list if a client is looking for one in the area. But it is both possible and advisable to go much further.

The Timothy Financial website is an example of how pricing can be used as a marketing tool, rather than as a mere disclosure item (see Figure 10). This graphic communicates the offering, fee model, and fee levels in one place. The prospective client sees what they will pay for the initial planning engagement, based on level of complexity.

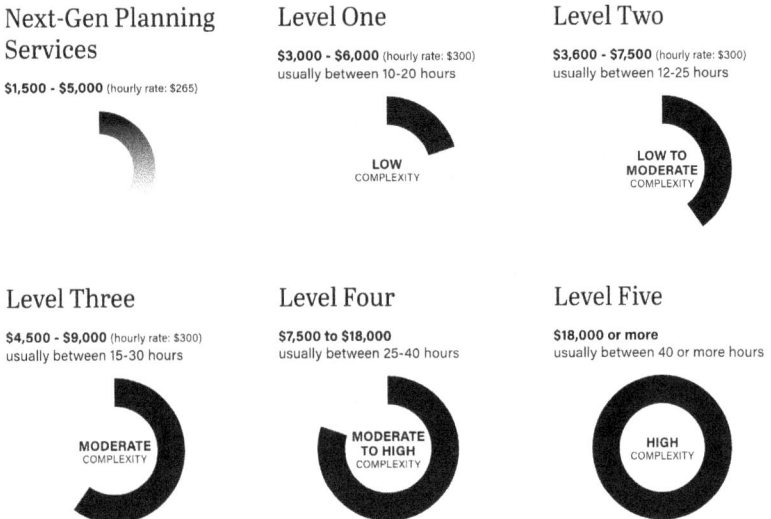

Next-Gen Planning Services

$1,500 - $5,000 (hourly rate: $265)

Level One

$3,000 - $6,000 (hourly rate: $300)
usually between 10-20 hours

LOW COMPLEXITY

Level Two

$3,600 - $7,500 (hourly rate: $300)
usually between 12-25 hours

LOW TO MODERATE COMPLEXITY

Level Three

$4,500 - $9,000 (hourly rate: $300)
usually between 15-30 hours

MODERATE COMPLEXITY

Level Four

$7,500 to $18,000
usually between 25-40 hours

MODERATE TO HIGH COMPLEXITY

Level Five

$18,000 or more
usually between 40 or more hours

HIGH COMPLEXITY

Figure 10: Presenting fees by linking hourly rate and effort.

Detractors of the hourly model point to the "salience" of quoting fees in dollars rather than on basis points. To be clear, there are clients who would rather not see the bill, and these would be better served by less prominent models.

For the hourly planner, this openness can actually be put to good use in the marketing phase. By exposing the prospect to the sticker shock early on, those who are genuinely a bad fit for the model will end the process and save everyone's time.

To those clients for whom this is not a deal breaker, the fees will simply communicate that the firm stands by its value.

Prospecting

Here is the current breakdown of new clients (by source of lead) at Timothy Financial:

- 35% from existing clients
- 15% from personal connections
- 20% from web search/NAPFA website
- 15% from other financial advisors ("I can't serve you but . . .")
- 15% from other professionals (CPA, attorney)

As you would expect, referrals from clients and personal connections make up the largest portion (50%). But a decent share (30%) comes from other advisors and professionals.

When cultivating relationships with CPAs and attorneys, there are a few points that an hourly planner should bear in mind. It's important to emphasize the flexibility of the hourly model, which is one of its greatest strengths. An hourly planner can be of potential service to a wider variety

"An hourly planner can be of potential service to a wider variety of clients than the traditional advisor."

of clients than the traditional advisor. This naturally multiplies the number of potential referrals from any source.

With a center of influence, sharing stories of work that you have done that a traditional advisor would normally *not* be involved with (for example, complex midlife situations with no liquidity event involved) is a way to illustrate this point. You will be the first advisor to come to mind when a similar situation arises.

Experience has shown that there can be some challenges to overcome with other professionals, such as CPAs. Mark has noticed that introducing himself as an hourly planner can initially provoke bewilderment. You should be prepared to answer a series of familiar questions:

- "Yes, we bill by the hour."
- "No, we don't do assets under management."
- "No, we don't have any affiliation with any other vendor."
- "No, we don't get referral fees. We just charge for our time."

Since hourly planning is still a rare phenomenon, the other party may assume that there must be something "off" about an advisor who elects to charge this way. The best antidote to this bewilderment is confidence. If you have the conviction that the hourly model is robust and fair, others will pick up on this and be reassured.

Initial Discussion

As noted, the hourly planner is likely to serve a more diverse group of clients than the typical advisor. Different aspects of the planning offering will be relevant to these various groups. Mark addresses this diversity in the initial meeting by sharing a list of typical reasons that clients work with him. He finds that at least one or two of these will resonate.

As an hourly advisor you can serve everyone, but you need to listen carefully so you can meet them where they are. Some clients will be looking for an advisor to validate a specific course of action. Others may have no clear idea how to proceed and will be looking for ideas.

Listening carefully means not necessarily taking the words at face value, but looking behind the words for the real reason they are seeking help. For example, sometimes it becomes clear that the client is looking for a back-up in case something happens to their spouse.

In many cases, establishing the reason that a client is seeking advice could be the entire aim of the conversation. Once the reason is found, the client is sold. But it is also worthwhile to establish a common understanding of what you have to offer before proceeding.

There is no single, right way to describe financial planning. A planner charging by the hour can claim (if needed) an added objectivity in not having a stake in the client's AUM balance, but apart from this, every planner will have their own version.

Approximately one-third of Mark's prospects approach him asking for something that they call investment advice. These are usually financial planning clients who do not have the vocabulary to articulate their broader needs beyond the portfolio.

In such cases, Mark responds, "Yes, we do give advice on investments. Let me tell you how." Then he describes the process of discovery, goal setting, analysis, and finally implementation. By the end of the discussion, such a prospect will understand that in order to be in a position to give good investment advice, the advisor must have the full picture of a client's situation and their plans for the future.

One final point: it is a good idea in the first meeting to establish an attorney-style client privilege relationship to signify a change in the relationship's status from prospect to client. In practical terms, establishing privilege could take the form of a payment of 50% of the initial engagement fee, plus the signing of a written agreement.

This will separate those who are serious from those who are just fishing. It also means that you can confidently reserve staff capacity for clients, rather than find yourself in the position of having to keep staff available while a potential client hesitates.

A Word on Discounts

The golden rule: **never discount an hourly rate**.

Negotiating on the rate is an admission that you are not worth what you say you are. It also implies that there is not a direct relationship between fees and value. Both of these admissions strike at the foundation of your financial and ethical stability.

Confidence is important when defending fees, but it is easily shaken. Particularly in the early stages of your career, you might ask yourself, "Am I really worth $300 per hour?" Well, the honest answer is, you're not. **You are worth considerably more.** But if you approach the pricing conversation with hesitance and embarrassment, what is the client supposed to think? They need your confidence to reassure them, especially if they have not experienced advice before.

> "Negotiating on the rate is an admission that you are not worth what you say you are."

If you are in any doubt, you should ask a client (when the relationship has had a chance to mature) if expectations were met and if the questions they brought to you were answered. In Mark's experience, the answer is almost invariably a resounding yes.

A competitor advertising a lower hourly rate is communicating, unintentionally of course, that the expertise being delivered is of a lower standard. Do not follow them!

Dealing with Negotiators

The simple logic of hourly is that it matches the fees paid to the value received and is therefore easy to explain. For clients actively seeking an hourly relationship, the fee discussion obviously presents no issues.

In 10% of cases, however, there may be some pushback. This is likely to happen if the client is a natural bargainer and would feel they had let themselves down if they omitted to negotiate. It is the more affluent clients who tend to be the negotiators. This is likely because the added complexity means that they also tend to need substantially more time as well as higher expertise (such as paying $50k in a given year), and hence have more to gain by getting you to trim the hourly rate.

Another form in which negotiation can manifest itself is an attempt to challenge the number of hours required. This is linked to a tendency among highly successful people to feel somewhat ashamed that they cannot do the job by themselves.

It makes little sense, as few rich and successful people choose to represent themselves in court, or complete their own tax returns. We see it as yet another indication of the underdeveloped status of financial planning in comparison with other professions.

As financial planning becomes better understood as a complex field of expertise, this should change. And over the course of an individual relationship, even a skeptical client will begin to perceive that advanced expertise is required.

Whatever the cause for equivocation, the client who negotiates is essentially requesting to pay less and receive the same amount of value. This is possible to do with cars, houses, and even companies. Why not—they think to themselves—with professional advice?

The key to responding to this strategy is to bring the focus back to the time-value relationship. As the golden rule of negotiation states: don't say no, say yes, if . . .

You can, for instance, respond by asking, "Of course we can lower the bill. Let's just agree on what to take out of the scope. Insurance? Investments?" To which the client will normally respond, "I want advice on all those areas," thus ending the negotiation themselves.

If the debate is around the quote for the initial (fixed) planning fee, you could offer to make the fee open-ended (in other words, depending on the actual time required). In this case, 99% of clients will opt for the firm quote.

If a client requests a lower hourly rate, the conversation can again pivot immediately to value, with an explanation that a lower rate comes with a less experienced advisor. Since no one wants the wrong advisor, this is normally the end of the conversation.

There are of course some hard cases who will attempt to dodge fees by piggybacking on calls with other clients from the same company, or persistently challenging the bill in an attempt to wear you down. Such cases are rare enough to be solved by politely explaining to the client that the relationship is unlikely to be fruitful if continued in this way. Ultimately, it may genuinely be a case of a mismatch in fee model, and therefore better to part ways.

Framing the Fee

By framing the fee correctly, it is often possible to avoid negotiation altogether.

The piecemeal nature of hourly fees, spread out over the course of a year, is itself a fantastic framing device. A complex client, who might blanch at committing to $30k up front for an as yet unrealized set of gains, instead has the feeling, "I always walk away with something," after each meeting.

An obvious reframing strategy is to compare the hourly fee to its AUM equivalent. While this is often a slam dunk argument in mathematical terms (particularly in the case of wealthy clients), it is not always effective.

Mark has a client with a net worth of $25 million who was used to paying his advisor on a percentage of AUM basis. One day, the client called to complain about a bill he had received for eight hours of work.

Even after a detailed discussion about the work involved, and being shown that his fee was the equivalent of a few basis points when calculated on an AUM basis, the client remained uncomfortable. The deadlock was finally broken when Mark asked the client to compare his hourly rate with the rate he paid his lawyer. This flipped a switch, and the client's objections vanished.

In this case, the change of mental frame was not numerical but categorical. The client had not categorized Mark's services as "professional," but as soon as he did so, the reference point became legal fees, and the problem was resolved.

As we write this book, hourly planning fees (which range between $100 and $600 per hour) are likely to be close enough to legal rates to be taken seriously, but not so high in comparison as to appear unreasonable.

Handling Crises

One other topic in relation to fees worth discussing is the client who is in a difficult situation. It is an unavoidable fact that large planning bills will often accompany times of upheaval in a client's life.

To avoid this larger payment coming as a surprise, transparency ahead of time can be helpful in such situations, particularly if the client in question has not worked with you long enough to develop an intuition regarding the fees they can expect for a given amount of effort.

One of Mark's clients, who had experienced a bereavement, called to say that she had received the latest bill and was happy to pay it, but would like to ask how much more work was likely needed. Mark responded that there was probably as much work remaining as had already been completed, and on receiving this perspective, the client thanked him for the clarification, and the matter was resolved. She subsequently requested assistance with a follow-on issue.

What if a client throws themselves at your mercy and/or implies that they expect you to waive your fees in view of their situation?

This is of course awkward, and there is no easy way to handle it. One way to respond would be the following: "We are absolutely prepared to waive our fees if clients do not see value in the service we are providing. If that's the case, it would probably make sense to

"Do not waive fees if you want to build a viable hourly planning business."

end our relationship here and see if we can find you another advisor. Alternatively, we are more than happy to spread out the payments on a monthly basis until the full amount is settled."

However you decide to respond, the bottom line remains the same: do not waive fees if you want to build a viable hourly planning business.

Establishing the Relationship

With the proposition and fee structure explained, the next step is for the advisor to communicate to the client how they will work together. The hourly advisor cannot assume that the client will automatically schedule a meeting twice yearly, or that they will want or need these meetings. This does not mean that they should leave it up to the client.

As we have said elsewhere, a passive approach will lead to a dysfunctional advisory relationship.

The ideal relationship is harder to describe, but is akin to a dance. There are "steps" (annual meetings/touchpoints), but the sequence is not rigidly choreographed. And in this analogy, it is the advisor and not the client who must lead.

On the subject of annual meetings, the advisor can say, "We typically meet with our clients on average once a year, just to make sure we stay on track. But we also customize our schedule to the needs of the client."

The ball is then in the client's court, and they are free to meet as many times as they like, or not at all. Typically, a client who is comfortable with their advisor will follow the advisor's guidance. It is therefore important that the advisor provide it.

If some time has gone by, and a client has not reached out, it is possible to ask a nonbillable staff member to phone or email to check back in. If everything is all right, there is no need for a meeting or a bill.

Building the Relationship

The flexibility of the hourly model allows the relationship to evolve at its own pace according to client situation and preference.

Mark remembers a client who started out on a light, once-a-year cadence. This annual meeting lasted a couple of hours, consisting mainly of the client running through a list of questions he had prepared.

As trust accumulated, Mark was in a position to say, "The questions you are asking me require me to look at your bigger picture." In other words, the next logical step was a financial plan, and with it a deeper and more value-generative discussion. Having drawn up the plan, Mark felt able to suggest that it was time to move to twice a year, and the client agreed without hesitation.

Over the course of interactions, the client internalizes the message, "If you work with me more, I will charge you more, but only if you see the value. If not, you will let me know by reducing the hours or going to zero."

Expanding the Relationship

Even with clients who are fully committed to planning for their financial goals, it may become clear that there is a chance to support on multigenerational issues.

Mark has noticed that the question, "What have you done to prepare your kids for their inheritance?" is almost invariably followed by an awkward silence. If trust has been established, the conversation then turns to planning for the next generation.

The advisor must intuit when sufficient trust has accumulated to propose the next step. All the while remembering that, while the advisor may lead, it's the client's choice whether to follow, find another dance partner, or leave the dance floor altogether.

The hourly firm does not have to worry about getting clients in the door. The focus instead should be getting the right clients in the door and ensuring that they do not have any misconceptions about the offer or the fee model that may harm their ability to receive the advice they need.

> "The hourly firm does not have to worry about getting clients in the door."

In the remaining three chapters, we'll be looking at the internal management of the firm, which is where the main challenges of running an hourly business are to be found.

PART 3

RUNNING THE FIRM

Chapter 7

Planning: Keeping It Real

Typically, an hourly firm will begin as a solo practice, established either by an entrepreneur who is new to the field or (more likely) the former employee of an established business.

For the new business owner, the hourly model allows greater precision when planning from year to year. This is because there is a direct, calculable link between work done, revenue earned, and employee capacity. Furthermore, historical data accumulate over time and allow forecasts to be made with a higher degree of certainty.

In this chapter, we'll give a sense of what this means in more concrete terms.

Starting Out

If you plan to start your own firm, it's advisable to have at least some practical experience in a financial planning role beforehand. At a minimum, you should aim to have the CFP® qualification or an equivalent that requires planning experience.

Needless to say, you also need the mindset of an entrepreneur. This, and a willingness to endure the skepticism of your advisor peers, not all of whom will appreciate the merits of the model you have chosen.

What will the first few years look like? No one knows, except that they will be challenging. But you can start with a plan.

To forecast revenues, the first step is to determine your rate. What you'll charge will depend on the complexity of the clients you intend to work with. At Timothy Financial, the hourly rates range from $300 (for advisors serving levels 1 and 2) $600 (for the firm founder).

Clearly, experience is a factor in determining the maximum client complexity you can handle. There is, however, no hard and fast correlation between years of experience and maximum complexity.

The time it takes to attain the ability to serve level 5 clients can be anywhere from three to ten years. Speed of progress depends on (1) **interest** in working with more complex clients and (2) **capacity** to learn.

Sometimes, a higher complexity client will take exception to being served by a comparatively young advisor. In this case, pairing the advisor with an older colleague can help to overcome the barrier.

Now let's dive into some illustrations.

The Lifestyle Practice

Morgan has worked for fifteen years at a boutique planning firm that specializes in ultra-high net worth families. He believes that he can serve a small number of ultra-high net worth clients on his own and decides to go solo. He chooses a rate of $450 per hour.

He plans to spend up to twelve weeks (one quarter) on vacation over the course of a year. In the remaining nine months, he aims to spend 60% of his time on billable work and 40% on prospecting and admin. He can therefore calculate what the revenue of the business will be when running at full speed.

Total hours in a working year	2,000[1]
Less 25% for vacation	(500)
Hours at work	1,500
Less 40% for other overhead	(600)
Hours available for clients	900
Potential revenue @ $450/hr	$405,000

Note 1: We use 2,000 hours rather than the more accurate 2,080 for the sake of rounder numbers in our calculations.

The rate of $450 is based on his experience (see chapter 5). As a cross-check, he notes that the forecast revenue is more than enough to cover his expenses and generate an acceptable profit margin, which he can use to fund his vacation time and other projects.

Morgan's plan makes sense given his history, situation, and aims. As an experienced, well-connected advisor, his network of COIs and planning colleagues provides an excellent source of referrals and new prospects, and his aim of supporting his lifestyle is clearly attainable.

The Growth Firm

Many advisors will not start in such a strong position as Morgan and will furthermore have ambitions to grow beyond a solo practice.

Let's take the example of Alex, who is planning to leave her current employer of seven years, two as a paraplanner and five as a junior advisor. She does not have substantial savings like Morgan, so she has more questions to answer. How long will it be before she can make rent? How long before she makes a profit? And how long before she can make her first professional hire?

A realistic plan will answer these questions and provide the confidence she needs to avoid the trap of accepting any client who will fog a mirror, at any rate they will accept! The first step is to calculate expected year-by-year revenue. She maps out her expected utilization for the first five years.

In her first year, she calculates that the majority of her time will be spent getting the business up and running. This includes administrative tasks (such as obtaining IT equipment) and of course marketing and prospecting activities to acquire her initial clients.

She estimates that in the first year her overall utilization (that is, the percentage of her time spent serving paying clients) will be 15% (= 300 hours), and this number will climb steadily as the business finds its feet.

She has heard from an experienced colleague that hourly planners, particularly those with management responsibilities, should target a utilization rate not much higher than 60%. Alex expects to reach this goal by year 5.

	Year 1	Year 2	Year 3	Year 4	Year 5
Utilization	15%	30%	45%	55%	60%
Hours	300 hrs	600 hrs	900 hrs	1,100 hrs	1,200 hrs

She sets her initial rate at $300 dollars. As per our advice in chapter 5, she plans also to raise her hourly rate by at least 10% every three years.

She can now calculate a revenue forecast.

	Year 1	Year 2	Year 3	Year 4	Year 5
Hours	300 hrs	600 hrs	900 hrs	1,100 hrs	1,200 hrs
Hourly rate	$300/hr	$300/hr	$300/hr	$350/hr	$350/hr
Revenue	$90,000	$180,000	$270,000	$385,000	$420,000

This is impressive growth, and Alex is confident she can achieve it. Given that she wants to grow the firm, her next question is when can she can hire a junior advisor to share the workload and train as a colleague.

This requires her to think about costs and profit margins. While the temptation may be to break even, a target margin is important for planning. A margin can serve as a shock absorber and as a fund for unexpected investments (for example, opportunistic hires).

Thinking ahead, a healthy profit margin also makes partnership an attractive goal for new employees. The prospect of additional compensation in later years provides a motivation to work hard during the early years, which is of course positive for the firm as well.

(To repeat a point we made in chapter 5, the target margin is not how you set the hourly rate. The hourly rate should remain fixed in any calculations for a given year, with the other factors falling into place around it.)

Let's assume that Alex is targeting a profit margin of 30%. She begins by calculating overheads, based on a combination of rental and other periodic costs. From there, she calculates what she can afford to pay in compensation and what will be left over in profits.

	Year 1	Year 2	Year 3	Year 4	Year 5
Revenue	$90,000	$180,000	$270,000	$385,000	$420,000
Overhead	$67,500	$80,000	$85,000	$90,000	$95,000
Salary	$22,500	$100,000	$135,000	$192,500	$210,000
Profit	$0	$0	$50,000	$102,500	$115,000

In her first year, it is a question of covering business and living expenses. By the second year, Alex can afford to pay herself a proper salary, and by the third, the business is making a modest profit.

By year 5, she is close to making her target profit margin of 30% and earning a salary that is higher than in her previous role.

A Note on Cost Structure

The hourly practice operates on a materially lower cost base than a firm that manages assets as a core part of its proposition. A firm that deals directly with client assets incurs significant yearly overhead in the form of expensive software subscriptions and more administrative staff.

> "The hourly firm can afford higher salaries and benefits for its staff and/or take a higher margin."

While an asset-managing firm might expect to pay up to 40% of its revenue in overhead costs, the hourly firm can target a range of 20 to 30%, depending on real estate expenses. Offering the same value to clients, but with a lower administrative burden, means that the hourly firm can afford higher salaries and benefits for its staff and/or take a higher margin.

Adding Staff

Now that Alex has a general sense of her future trajectory, she is able to plan recruiting. She wants to hire at the first available opportunity. This appears to be year 3, the first year of profitability.

Modeling this requires her to estimate the utilization, hourly rate, and adjusted overhead for a second employee, seen in the following calculations.

	Year 1	Year 2	Year 3	Year 4	Year 5
Utilization					
Advisor 1	15%	30%	45%	55%	60%
Advisor 2			10%	30%	40%
Staff hours					
Advisor 1	300 hrs	600 hrs	900 hrs	1,100 hrs	1,200 hrs
Advisor 2			200 hrs	600 hrs	800 hrs

	Year 1	Year 2	Year 3	Year 4	Year 5
Hourly rates					
Advisor 1	$300/hr	$300/hr	$300/hr	$350/hr	$350/hr
Advisor 2			$200/hr	$200/hr	$200/hr
Staff billing					
Advisor 1	$90,000	$180,000	$270,000	$385,000	$420,000
Advisor 2	$0	$0	$40,000	$120,000	$160,000
Totals					
Revenue	$90,000	$180,000	$310,000	$505,000	$580,000
Hours	300 hrs	600 hrs	1,100 hrs	1,700 hrs	2,000 hrs
Margins					
Overhead	$67,500	$80,000	$100,000	$116,000	$125,000
Salary	$22,500	$100,000	$186,000	$252,500	$290,000
Profit margin	$0	$0	$24,000	$136,500	$165,000

In this example, Alex decides to start the new employee on an hourly rate of $200, assuming a lower workload to begin with (10% utilization). The new employee will be able to share the administrative tasks, creating space for Alex to train and supervise.

The employee's salary will be funded in part by the additional revenue and in part by a sacrifice in profit for year 3. This loss in profit will be recovered almost immediately in the following year.

Planning at Scale

Let's go further into Alex's future and take a look at how she might plan for a mature practice with multiple employees. In the early years, planning is mainly about reaching profitability. In later years, it is a question of managing capacity. Capacity problems will inevitably result in stressed advisors and potentially lost revenues. The only solution is hiring more staff.

Hiring and training new staff takes time, so Alex needs to be aware of capacity constraints *before* they become an issue.

First, let's look at how Alex's firm did in the latest year:

	Last year			
	Hours	**Utilization**	**Rate/hr**	**Revenue**
Founder	1,250	63%	$600	$750,000
Senior Partner	1,200	60%	$450	$540,000
Senior Advisor	1,000	50%	$300	$300,000
Junior Advisor	650	33%	$265	$172,250
Junior Advisor	485	24%	$265	$128,525
Total	4,585	46%	$412	$1,890,775

The firm has experienced growth in demand (= total billable hours) of approximately 10% for the past few years and expects this to continue into next year.

With current utilization below 50%, it appears as if the firm could comfortably manage another 450 hours or so.

This is where the concept of billability becomes useful. Like utilization, billability is a measure of billable hours. But instead of dividing by the total number of hours in a year, it is divided by the number of hours available for clients (see Figure 11).

Total hours	Available hours	Key metrics
Planned Overhead	Nonbillable hours	Utilization $= \dfrac{\text{Billable hours}}{\text{Total hours}}$
Hours available for client work	Billable hours	Billability $= \dfrac{\text{Billable hours}}{\text{Available hours}}$

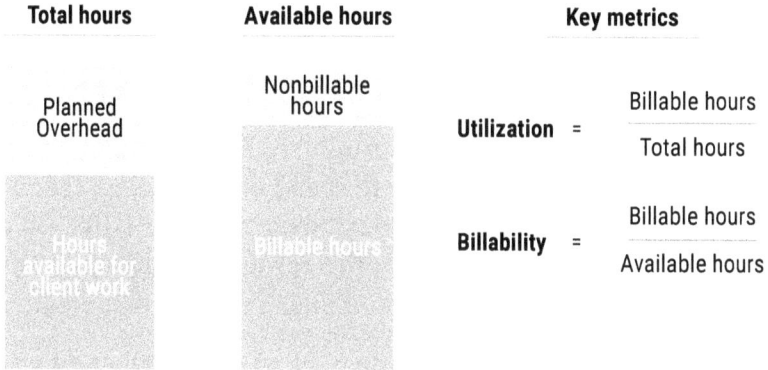

Figure 11: Utilization and Billability provide different perspectives on firm financials.

In the case of Morgan, you will recall the number of available hours was 900 (total hours less planned overhead). For Alex's business, the default assumption is that advisors will have 1,200 hours (or 60% of total hours) available for client work.

Because billability measures the relationship of actual versus potential hours, it allows us to measure capacity more accurately. Let's compare the two measures.

	Hours	**Utilization** (divide by 2,000)	**Billability** (divide by 1,200)
Founder	1,250	63%	104%
Senior Partner	1,200	60%	100%
Senior Advisor	1,000	50%	83%
Junior Advisor	650	33%	54%
Junior Advisor	485	24%	40%
Total	4,585	46%	76%

Viewed through this lens, the capacity situation becomes clearer. Alex (the founder) is clearly maxed out, as is the senior partner (her original first hire).

Furthermore, the senior partner plans to redirect 100 hours of his time away from client work next year to spend on HR issues. This reduces the denominator, or available hours, from 1,200 to 1,100. Billability will therefore remain at 100% for this resource, while utilization will drop from 60% to 55%.

The senior advisor is at 83%, but on track to reach 100% next year. The two junior advisors have capacity, but are not underutilized considering their respective stages of development.

Assuming an increase in hours from 4,585 to 5,000, Alex maps out the following projection for next year.

	Next year			
	Hours	**Utilization**	**Billability**	**Revenue**
Founder	1,250	63%	104%	$750,000
Senior Partner	1,100	55%	100%	$495,000
Senior Advisor	1,200	60%	100%	$360,000
Junior Advisor	850	43%	71%	$225,250
Junior Advisor	600	30%	50%	$159,000
Total	5,000	50%	85%	$1,989,250

In this scenario, revenue grows by approximately 5% ($1,890,775 → $1,989,250), and firm billability increases to 85%, leaving 15% additional capacity.

15% may feel like a decent amount of leeway, but in this case it is mostly junior capacity, which may not be sufficient to handle a complex caseload (such as a sudden influx of levels 4 and 5 clients).

A general rule of thumb is to start the hiring process before the firm crosses the 80% mark. Given that it takes twelve to eighteen months to train a new planner, Alex should therefore be looking to make a new hire in the coming six months.

Effect of Discounts

We have already stressed in earlier chapters the importance of maintaining price integrity by charging what you are worth and avoiding discounts. Let's examine the effect of lower fees on Alex's business, taking the latest year as an example.

Hours billed	4,585
Average rate/hr	$412
Revenues	$1,890,775
Costs	$1,323,543
Net profit	$567,233
Margin %	30%

The following shows the effect of price decreases on profitability. As with any fixed-cost business, the impact of any price decrease is magnified, with a 30% decrease in fees ($412 → $289) eliminating 100% of the profits.

Average rate/hr	Fee reduction	Profit	Profit reduction
$412	0%	$567,233	0%
$392	-5%	$472,694	-17%
$371	-10%	$378,155	-33%
$351	-15%	$283,616	-50%
$309	-25%	$94,539	-83%
$289	-30%	$0	-100%

It is feasible to discount in other businesses, but not in an hourly one. You have been warned!

Strategic Goals

Beyond year-to-year planning and budgeting, there needs to be a strategic vision. This could be the domain of the founder, a senior partner, or the senior leadership as a whole. The vision will entail activities that are not part of the ordinary business of the firm, which require additional resources to accomplish.

These could include new approaches to training and marketing, scouting for new office locations, redesigning client service, rebuilding the tech stack, or taking a more intentional approach to firm culture.

The point is that any strategic plan, no matter how inspired, must be conceived within the realistic constraints of the time and resources available to carry them out. The hourly firm can quantify these constraints precisely, with a time and resource budget that provides a limit on additional activities. Time diverted from billable work will result in lower revenues that must be made up from elsewhere.

Thus Tim (junior advisor) can take time out to study for an advanced tax qualification (40 hours), but Alex will likely have to shelve her plans for a part-time lecturer position at Texas A&M (80 hours).

This unforgiving process may mean that many good ideas are set aside. But a planning process grounded in reality has a higher likelihood of approving plans that will survive.

The Growth Imperative

Most advice firms do not grow beyond ten employees—typically the founder and a group of loyal staff. Aside from cases such as Morgan, where the aim is to remain a solo practitioner, we predict a different future for the hourly planning enterprise.

Alex's model of doing business is far closer to that of a professional service firm. In such firms, equity-owning partners leverage junior employees, who work for a salary on the understanding that, longer term, they themselves have a decent shot at partnership and profit participation.

> "Unlike the asset-hunter, Alex faces a limitless ocean of demand—the untapped hourly market."

This marks a departure from the eat-what-you-kill approach, which generates a series of loosely agglomerated fiefdoms, whose holders have little incentive to collaborate or foster the next generation.

Unlike the asset-hunter, Alex faces a limitless ocean of demand— the untapped hourly market. Since there is no additional revenue without additional work in the hourly model, she needs to develop juniors in order to grow. She will therefore be looking for ambitious, professionally minded advisors, with a decent stretch of road ahead of them to justify the professional "earning curve."

With the employees who are attracted by the professional model, Alex is not simply creating a new firm, she is creating a new profession.

Scalability

In chapter 1 we referenced the myth that hourly firms are unscalable, promising that we would address this question more fully later. It is important here to draw a distinction between financial planning and portfolio management (managing assets). The two are often delivered together, but are separate activities.

Portfolio management is a scalable service, since a single strategy can be used on a one-to-many basis (that is, across multiple clients). In such a case, every additional dollar invested brings the advisor more revenue at no additional cost. Planning is fundamentally a case-by-case discipline and hence does not share this property.

The hourly firm scales initially through leveraging fixed-cost employees by delegating overhead activities to free up revenue-earning time for more experienced advisors.

The second stage of scaling comes through leveraging processes and methodologies, which can be deployed on a one-to-many basis—just like software, the classic scalable good.

Timothy Financial's five levels approach to assessing complexity is an example of a scalable methodology. It provides a common vocabulary that enables clarity and efficiency across a network of advisors, with no constraints on network size.

Alex's firm can open an office in Phoenix, or Chicago, without having to reinvent the processes she developed with her original team in Austin. She looks forward to the day when she no longer knows every client by name, a sign that the business has truly begun to scale.

As we will see in the next chapter, an hour-by-hour view of what is done, for how long, and by whom puts the hourly firm in a stronger position to build, document, and propagate such processes across teams.

Chapter 8

Management: Let the Data Do the Talking

Moving on from the founder's big picture, we now turn to the realm of the manager, the day-to-day operations of the firm. In an hourly firm, where staff track their time and activities, the manager has access to an enviable treasure trove of data.

These data can be viewed on three levels:

- **Lens 1**: In the aggregate, how the firm is spending its time
- **Lens 2**: Advisor level, how advisors spend their time versus the firm average
- **Lens 3**: Client level, what each client is receiving, and how much and from whom

These lenses are helpful insofar as they help the manager understand two aspects: **processes** and **people**. Issues in either of these areas impact the firm's ability to grow profitably.

Let's look at each area in turn and see how the data can be used to ensure profitable growth.

Processes

Using the Data

Hourly revenue, logically, depends on the ability to manage time. Failure to manage time will show up in the data via low or declining billability, either at the individual level or across the staff as a whole.

It's important to bear in mind that data are only useful to the extent they are used. Here is a story that illustrates this point.

Mark knew a law firm owner who had his staff track their time for the purposes of billing clients (Lens 3), but did not use the data for broader management purposes (Lenses 1 and 2). One day, he decided to look at the timesheet data more closely. He found that, out of a firm of five lawyers, he, by himself, accounted for 60% of the total billable hours.

"A busy office atmosphere can give the misleading impression of general productivity."

His junior partner was responsible for 30%, and the other three associates together accounted for only 10%. One of these associates billed only sixty to ninety minutes per working day. He also tended to rush his work, meaning that the head partner had to spend time correcting the mistakes.

The status quo was clearly inefficient, with the firm owner trapped in a classic manager's dilemma ("It's faster to do it myself"). As a result, the junior resources were operating below capacity, and he had no time to develop them through mentorship.

A busy office atmosphere can give the misleading impression of general productivity. Employees are unlikely to advertise the fact that they feel underworked or lost. As a result, seemingly bizarre situations like this can persist without anyone being fully aware.

All the data were being collected to diagnose the problem. What was missing was management.

Appropriate Benchmarks

If you are reviewing the data, you need something to compare against. For example, what is low utilization? You can judge whether an employee is underutilized based on their years of service. Studying past utilization figures for advisors at different levels of experience will provide a baseline.

If utilization is persistently low across the board (with excessive overhead or nonbillable activities), this could be due to insufficient demand or inefficient processes.

In the case of hourly firms that have been in business for two to four years or longer, lack of client demand is unlikely to be the issue. By this stage, most firms are backed up with new prospects.

A sudden surge in new prospects will lead to a temporary spike in nonbillable time, resulting from nonbillable prospecting. This, coupled with the 80% threshold mentioned in the previous chapter, is generally an advance warning that the firm will need to hire new talent.

Low utilization across the board is more likely to be related to inefficient processes. Problems related to processes typically result from how things are done (= efficiency) or what things are done (= effectiveness).

Efficiency

Generally, the quickest wins can be found by reviewing processes and tasks that we know are necessary but take longer than we would like. In every case, the problem can be identified in the data, and the data will also show subsequently if the solution has worked.

Faster Processes

In the case of a process that is common, necessary, and time-consuming, the manager can apply the following approach:

1. **Ascertain the current time taken:** This can be found in the timesheet data.
2. **Set a target time:** This could be initially based on intuition and refined based on experience.
3. **Identify the pinch-points:** May require discussion with the team and/or further investigation by the manager.

Sometimes step 1 is all that is necessary. That is to say, the manager, by simply causing a KPI to be observed, influences the behavior of the team in the desired direction.

At Timothy Financial, the client onboarding process appeared to be taking too long to complete. Records showed that onboarding took on average sixty-nine calendar days from start to finish. The team had a feeling it could be shorter, so it was added as a KPI to the list of items being tracked.

Without any explicit target or changes to the process, the awareness that the number was being tracked was enough to bring the onboarding time progressively downward. Eventually, it was cut by more than a third to forty-two days.

In this case, the decline happened over a few years. No doubt the effect could have been achieved quicker if the process had been consciously redesigned. But the point is that in some cases awareness is enough to gamify the process of optimization.

Delegation

Inefficiency could also be a case of the right things being done in the right way by the wrong person.

Founders who begin as solo practitioners have a particular tendency to under delegate, for example spending time poring over expense receipts when it is the office manager's job, or could be delegated to a junior with a lower utilization target.

Effectiveness

Whereas efficiency is about how well one does things, effectiveness is a question of what one does. This often involves eliminating needless tasks to make room for important ones.

Eliminating Tasks

Attempting to calculate financial return on effort is advisable with billable work and short-term prospecting activities. Not all important activities generate revenue immediately or at all. Such activities should at least sustain revenue (for example, office admin) or have some prospect of generating revenue in the long term (such as business development, training in core skills).

Some activities, such as reading the *Wall Street Journal* for thirty minutes every day, are clearly a poor use of time when measured against this standard. Once identified in a timesheet, they should be discontinued or moved outside of business hours.

If too few clients are in the pipeline, it is a sign that more time should be allotted to prospecting and marketing activities. This is, once again, a case of looking at the current allocation, setting a target, and making room in the calendar.

Periodically, the manager can examine the current split of time by firm/team/resource, ask where it should be, and figure out what the firm can outsource, automate, or eliminate altogether.

Instituting Processes

In the previous chapter, we talked about process design as a means of scaling the hourly firm. It is the job of the manager to design, implement, and test these processes. The aim is to ensure that the right tasks get done every time.

Let's take a concrete example. When a prospect calls Timothy Financial for the first time, the staff member taking the call will follow a predetermined script that covers the following steps:

- "What led you to call us?"
- "Let me briefly introduce the firm."
- "Based on what you've told us, this is your complexity level."
- "This would be the initial fee range."
- "The most appropriate advisor for you would be . . ."
- "Would you like to schedule an appointment?"

This scripted approach to the initial touchpoint illustrates two important items:

- While not billable, the first touchpoint with a client is important. To be safely delegated, it must be planned, scripted, and repeatable.
- The process is handled by the client service team and not the advisor pool. This helps to maximize billable time for the advisor and sets the precedent that an advisor's time is worth paying for.

> "Any process that is valuable and repeatable is scalable."

Any process that is valuable and repeatable is scalable, as all staff who have the process will perform the task in the same way. This approach fulfills the manager's guiding principle of freeing up as much revenue-generating time for revenue-generating resources as possible, without sacrificing the client experience.

How would such a process come about?

A series of datapoints on the manager's dashboard, showing a general decline in billability during periods of heavy onboarding activity, could provide the opportunity to reexamine and redesign the status quo to address the issue.

Digging into this low billability might reveal that advisors are spending nontrivial amounts of time manning the phones. Advisors might counter by emphasizing the importance of making a good first impression, which would in turn lead to a discussion about what the ideal first impression looks like, which could then be scripted and delegated.

After instituting a new process like the approach just described, the manager should be able to see higher billability ensuing as a direct result of the new prospect introduction protocol.

> "Repeatable, teachable processes are good candidates for automated and workflow-based solutions."

The manager will continue to seek other routine work that can be removed from the senior advisors, such as implementation work, data entry, and so on. When this is optimized, the next step is to look at potential ways to free up the client service team. Repeatable, teachable processes are good candidates for automated workflow-based solutions. These take up zero hours on the timesheet and can be relied upon to operate with 100% accuracy.

Time management is a never-ending game with clear rules and an impartial referee. And cash prizes!

People

The "product" of an hourly firm is expertise. As expertise requires experts, without the right people, there is no product. This may sound obvious, but many firms trade on transferred or associative value (for example, the name of the founder).

As hourly advisors serve clients in an ensemble, resource management can be and often is a complex task. When a single client is served by a team of three or four advisors, the correct combination of skillsets is important. The skillsets of these resources moreover are continuously morphing and developing, and most will have the ambition to progress further.

The manager needs to be able to think about resources systematically, as there is a lot to manage.

Training and Teaming

In his book *Managing the Professional Service Firm*, David Maister sets out a framework for thinking about different kinds of professional engagement. He draws a distinction between three types of work, which he calls Procedural, Grey Hair, and Brains.

- Procedural work is deterministic and process-driven. In a law firm, it would be handled by junior staff (traditionally in the UK, lawyers in prestigious magic circle law firms spend their first year manning the photocopier).

- Grey Hair projects require experience to deliver effectively, with resources who can say "I've done this before." In planning parlance, these might be low to medium complexity clients.

- Brains projects require creativity to deliver, as they tend to present problems that have not been seen before. Such unique problems are common with highly complex planning clients.

It so happens that the three main categories of team at Timothy Financial are arranged according to Maister's three dimensions.

- **Client service:** This team handles Procedural work. Examples would include assisting clients with data gathering, implementation (such as data input) and so on. These tasks are critical, but repeatable, and therefore teachable.

- **Advisors for levels 1–4**: Handle Grey Hair problems, which, being familiar, typically elicit a narrow range of solutions.
- **Advisors for level 5**: Handle Brains problems, which may have multiple solutions depending on the planner.

Every employee, no matter what their career plans are, starts out in the client service team, carrying out procedural work. Not only does this ensure that young advisors can contribute from day one, it also gives them a holistic view of how the firm works. While contributing in a basic capacity on planning engagements, they have an opportunity to learn from Grey Hair advisors by observing the thought process and interactions with clients.

Mark has noticed there is a natural fork in the road after the initial years of training, where an advisor must decide whether to stay on the client service team, move into the Grey Hair zone of levels 1 through 4 or move into the Brains arena of level 5 clients (see Figure 12). Since the first group (levels 1-4) is numerous, and the second group (level 5) is highly remunerative, there is no real reason to favor one or the other.

Figure 12: Everyone begins in client service, but many paths are possible.

It is normally possible to tell which group an advisor falls into by observing the way they process decisions. But it is important for this preference to be known, not just for the sake of the individual advisor's career, but for the structure of the firm.

As stated earlier, advisors on a team work in an ensemble fashion, with the lead advisor beginning as the main point of contact for the client and progressively delegating more of the work to the midlevel and junior advisors on the team. The ensemble dimensions are key to the culture of the firm and its profitability.

Rather than jealously guarding clients and hoarding tasks, which is common in an eat-what-you-kill environment, the partners of an hourly firm are incentivized to "push down" as much work as possible. Additional revenues generate higher profits for the partners of the firm, and so the more fully and efficiently resources are deployed, the higher the profitability. (For a detailed discussion of this process, chapter 1 of *Managing the Professional Service Firm*, referenced here, is essential reading.)

If a lead advisor accounts for 25% or less of the hours billed to a given engagement, with the remainder divided up among four advisors of varying seniority, this is a sign that the lead advisor has succeeded in letting go, and that the team is functioning properly.

When a team reaches a certain size, one of the newly promoted senior advisors can break out and establish another team in the area they wish to focus on. Alternatively, a senior advisor may choose to remain in the team and nurture junior talent, rather than seek a team leadership role.

Hiring and Compensation

What should you be looking for in an hourly planner?

The table stakes are similar to any reputable planning firm, with a CFP° qualification the minimum educational requirement to become an advisor (though not necessarily an employee). The firm should expect to pay for coursework and testing, as well as offering study time during working hours.

As hourly work is demanding and reliant on the ability to solve problems based on expertise, an intellectual frame of mind and passion to learn is important. When the tax law changes, for instance, you need to be motivated to get on top of the details and implications. Otherwise, you are likely to be overwhelmed and ultimately fail to serve your clients appropriately.

As indicated elsewhere, being a good salesperson is not a key requirement, unless you are hiring specifically for a networking-oriented role that is focused exclusively on business development. It is a fact that some advisors are not cut out for life in an hourly planning firm. It's obviously ideal to spot this before making the hire, and much of the time it will be clear.

But, if not, the problems will sooner or later make themselves known in the manager's dashboard and can be addressed in short order.

> "The business is a product of its nonbillable time as much as its billable time, as each enables the other."

How should compensation work?

While traditionally financial advice firms have favored revenue or asset-based compensation systems, an hourly firm is best served by a system of salaries, bonuses (not incentives), and profit sharing for those elected partner. This is similar to the model espoused by other professional organizations and is also increasingly common among financial advice firms who wish to foster a more collaborative environment.

One further point to bear in mind is that client service team members can and should be considered eligible for partnership as well as advisors. The business is a product of its nonbillable time as much as its billable time, as each enables the other.

A final note, before we close the chapter, on the role of a manager. The manager could appear from this discussion to operate as a police officer, constantly pitted in semi-comedic style against the reckless antics of staff who refuse to get in line.

The fact is that a manager has no time to perform an invasive role like this, nor is it necessary, because 95% of the "policing" is conducted by the employees themselves, who naturally aspire to meet their objectives, which happen to be clearer by virtue of being time-monitored.

> "The ultimate 'manager' is the hourly mindset that naturally guides the actions of all employees in an established hourly firm."

We'll address the practical business of time-tracking in the next chapter. For now, it's important to recognize that the management of an hourly firm is in reality a distributed responsibility, and the ultimate "manager" is the hourly mindset that naturally guides the actions of all employees in an established hourly firm.

Chapter 9

Measurement: Tracking Your Most Valuable Asset

So much of the success of an hourly firm is down to the ability to measure reality, accurately. And as seen in the previous chapters, when you can quantify reality, you can alter it. In this final chapter, we look at the nitty-gritty of what it takes to implement the ideas we've been discussing.

Basic Analysis

An hourly firm should, as a bare minimum, understand how much of its time is spent on billable work. This view, though simple enough, allows you to identify many of the potential issues we discussed in the previous chapter, which mainly stem from poor time allocation.

At a click of a button, you can also see who has contributed work to a specific client case, uncovering issues of underdelegation and underexposure (see Figure 13).

Employee / Firm View   **Client-level view**

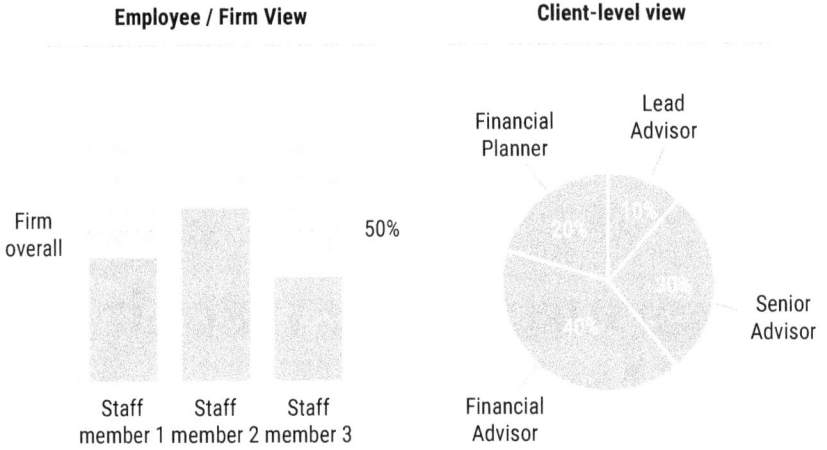

Firm overall   50%

Financial Planner   Lead Advisor

Senior Advisor

Staff member 1   Staff member 2   Staff member 3   Financial Advisor

Figure 13: Knowing what time is billable can help diagnose fundamental issues.

And of course, as already covered, you can compare the productivity levels of various employees against where you would expect them to be (see Figure 14).

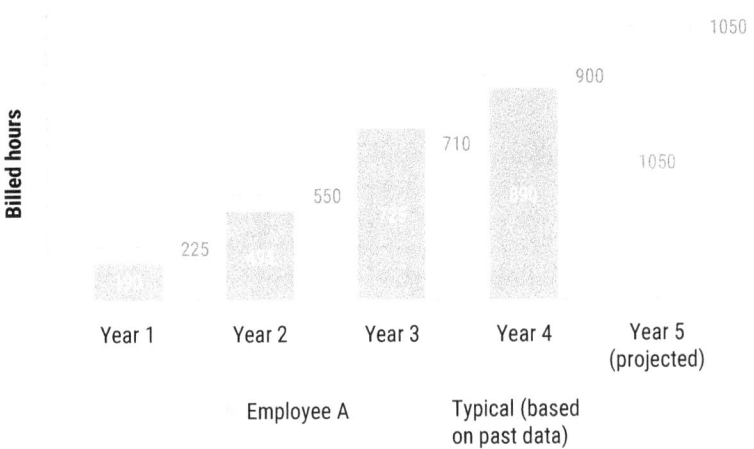

1050

900

710

550

225

1050

Year 1   Year 2   Year 3   Year 4   Year 5 (projected)

Employee A   Typical (based on past data)

Figure 14: Past data make it possible to benchmark a new employee's progress.

The next step is to dig deeper, creating further categories within the billable and nonbillable dimensions, unlocking a new cache of strategic data.

Time Categories

How a firm's employees spend their time is at the discretion of the business owner. But in order to make the decision, and see that it is followed, an owner needs more nuanced terms.

Categories are descriptive headings under which your team can classify the various blocks of activity they spend time on during a given day. A time category could refer to any activity, but will typically be one that accounts for a material quantity of the team's time.

Perhaps counterintuitively, the nonbillable categories are often the most useful. This is because the nonbillable activities of a firm are typically the least well understood. They include the activities that power the firm's growth and, hence, also contain the "unknown unknowns" that are silently draining the firm's profitability.

There is no universally correct set of nonbillable categories. They will and should alter and merge over time.

Here, by way of example, is how Timothy Financial categorizes its time.

Billable time is split into two categories:

1. **Meetings:** direct interaction with the client, face-to-face or by phone
2. **Counsel:** preparation and follow-up in between meetings

If a client is new, this is also noted in the data. Since there are no assets to track, it allows the firm to keep a record of new versus existing business (an important ratio for an hourly enterprise).

Nonbillable time is divided into the following seven categories:

1. **Marketing:** outbound efforts to proactively reach new clients and COIs
2. **Prospecting:** responding to inbound inquiries from new referrals
3. **Personal:** when an employee needs to carve out time for family or other issues not directly related to work

4. **New-hire training:** recorded to provide data on how much time is required to onboard a new employee

5. **Business planning:** covers meetings and sessions to discuss the strategy of the firm or other management-level decisions

6. **Continuing education:** webinars, studying for qualifications, reading industry publications and so on

7. **Admin:** a general catch-all bucket for overhead activities not considered significant enough to have their own category

Guidelines for Making Categories

To repeat, there is no categorization system that is right for all firms. Even a set of categories that is correct for a specific firm at a given time will change as the business changes. While there are no universal categories, there are some useful guidelines to produce a workable set.

Don't create a category without an objective. Time-tracking for its own sake is, ironically, a waste of time. A category should be created in order to test a hypothesis or turn a feeling into a fact.

For example, there was an advisor who attended Rotary events as a way to combine prospecting activity with charitable outreach. When he reviewed the results at the end of the year, he saw that he had spent 400 hours on Rotary activities and gained two clients as a result. Calculating the value of this time at $250 per hour, each new client cost around $50,000 in business development expenses!

"Time-tracking for its own sake is, ironically, a waste of time. A category should be created in order to test a hypothesis or turn a feeling into a fact."

Following this review, he might have reduced the time spent on Rotary events to 50 hours per year going forward and devoted 350 hours to more focused business development activities. Without testing his hypothesis, he might well have continued much longer before realizing the error.

Build the categories *with* your team. It may be tempting for the founder, as the main strategic thinker, to create the list of categories alone on a weekend and deliver it to the team as a *fait accompli*.

There are two reasons why creating the categories should be a bottom-up, team-based process, rather than a top-down, management-based one. In the first place, the whole team will be required to work with the new categories, day in and day out. Understanding and buy-in are key to ensuring that the categories are used consistently or at all. This is especially the case if time-tracking is an unfamiliar process to the employees in question.

Second, the task of creating the categories is difficult—more art than science—and the more perspectives that are available, the better the result will be. The founder may be completely unaware of certain activities, and the brainstorming exercise will by itself bring important unknowns to light about the running of the firm.

The process of reviewing and updating the categories after they have been in use for some time should also be a team activity. Reviewing the results every year as a group, for example, will stimulate important discussions about potential improvements to the business and help highlight necessary changes to the categories themselves.

Don't use more than ten categories. While it is a good idea to start broad, the final list of categories should be no more than ten (pro tip: if you want to end up at ten, aim for eight).

If a category accounts for less than 5% of total time, it is probably not worth tracking. Unless, of course, you have a strategic aim to increase this percentage to a more significant level. Whatever number of categories you agree on, agree to keep the total number constant going forward. If a new category is added, another should be retired to make room for it.

Why is this level of stringency necessary? Surely more categories means deeper insights? The reality is that creating too many categories will result in a system that is hard to work with and difficult to interpret. Furthermore, a bloated list is an indication that the brainstorming process ended too early and that not enough thought has been put into the hypotheses that are to be tested. This will lead to an increased amount of effort to gather data that is harder to make sense of.

The ultimate enforcer of this rule (and the most likely person to break it) is the founder. Be warned!

Starting from a Blank Page

Okay, so you are in the brainstorming session. The whiteboard is ready, and the team is caffeinated. How does one create a list of categories from scratch?

Build a Long List

The aim should initially be to get as many ideas on the board as possible. One way to generate a list of categories is to begin by thinking through a typical day, week, and month as a team, with each individual asking, "What did I do?"

The result will be a long, unstructured list of tasks, which include highly detailed activities such as responding to emails, call with prospect, and ordering new office supplies.

Group and Label

Most items will naturally fall into similar groups. The trick is to identify the item that is at the highest level of abstraction (the one that describes all the others). This item is the name of the category.

For example, responding to emails might be grouped along with making trades under the category of client service. Call with prospect and lunch with COI might fall under under the category of business development, and so on. Figure 15 illustrates this process with some basic examples.

Long list	Key steps	Categorized
• Restocking the coffee machine		**Office Admin**
		Restocking the coffee machine
• Team meeting		Team meeting
• Handling new inquiries	1. How are the items related?	**Prospecting**
		Active outreach to COIs
	2. What term describes the relationship?	
• Active outreach to COIs		Handling new inquiries
• Recruiting		
• Interviewing		**Recruiting**
		Interviewing
• …		…

Figure 15: Categories group the long list by theme and level of abstraction.

Prioritize and Simplify

You will almost certainly end up with too many categories. The next challenge—and the most valuable part of the process—will be to identify the categories you are most interested in or, in other words, which categories would benefit from scrutiny.

This could include an activity that is a priority for the coming year (let's say marketing), or an activity that is perceived to take too much of everyone's time (such as admin).

Categories that do not make the cut can be grouped together into the final catch-all category. If one of these discarded categories later turns out to be important, it can be broken out on its own in future iterations.

Set Objectives

If each category has a reason for tracking it, the final step should be to articulate a commitment or prediction. For example, if a new marketing category has been introduced, there should be a target for the coming quarter (for example, 400 hours) that the team commits to. At the next quarterly meeting, it will be possible to see if the target has been met.

If there is a clear need to reduce exposure to an existing category, once again, a maximum target threshold can be set and progress measured in subsequent meetings.

In the case of evergreen categories (such as client meetings), clear, quantitative KPIs can be set at a firm and individual level. Deviations from the goals that have been set will stimulate a helpful discussion as to why.

Review and Refine

Although the number of categories should not grow over time, as mentioned earlier, the categories themselves should change to reflect the priorities of the firm.

One year, at Timothy Financial, the team suspected that the firm had become overly reliant on inbound leads. This was when the decision was taken to split business development into two categories: prospecting (responding to inbound leads) and marketing (outbound lead generation, reaching out to COIs).

When the data were revealed, the overreliance hypothesis turned out to be correct. There was a significant skew toward passive prospecting, highlighting the need to take a more systematic approach to business development and providing a way to measure subsequent progress.

Tools for Time-Tracking

When it comes to tools, there are no common practices as yet. Some pioneers in the field of time-tracking have gotten by with Excel or even a pen and paper and a stopwatch.

Compared with creating a good list of categories, selecting a time-tracking software comes a distant second in terms of importance. A useful tool will not redeem a poorly thought through system of categorization.

That said, if you are looking for dedicated time-tracking software, you are in luck. The concept may be new in financial planning, but the practice of time-tracking is increasingly common not only in business life but also in the realm of personal productivity apps.

We won't attempt to give a survey of the various possibilities here. The only real way to determine the tool that is right for your team is to research some options (at whatever point in the future you are reading this) and experiment with one or two.

To help you, here are some considerations to bear in mind while examining options.

Ease of Use

When looking for a software solution, functionality (the number of features) should probably not be your priority, as time-tracking is not rocket science. On a given day, you mark the beginning of an activity by selecting the relevant category, and note the end by selecting a new one. A timer running in the background captures the time and records it automatically.

Rather than breadth of functionality, it is probably best to select for ease of use above everything else.

> "Minor inconveniences multiply across a firm and accumulate over time."

Even minor inconveniences multiply across a firm and accumulate over time, causing administrative drag and needless employee stress. There is a tendency among some solution developers to prioritize functionality over ease of use, so be sure to experience using the tool for at least a full day before committing.

Integration

The other important aspect to bear in mind, though secondary, is how well the time-tracking system integrates with your existing tech suite and, in particular, your billing system. If you are wedded to a particular billing system, this may help to narrow your choices.

That said, this consideration is likely to become less relevant as the nature of software changes over time and systems become increasingly interoperable. Eventually, you may be in a position to build your own customized time-tracking solution.

Manual vs. Automated

Some emerging solutions aim to detect what a user is doing and categorize their actions automatically. The rationale for this approach is to eliminate the potential for human error and also save time and energy.

We would recommend against pursuing this route for the near term at least. General artificial intelligence is a long way off, and until then, human judgment is likely needed. Most categories are separated by qualitative or subjective boundaries and so require a certain level of human intuition. It's not easy to explain to a computer the difference between prospecting and marketing.

Furthermore, the process of consciously attributing your time accounts for much of its value (see the onboarding example in chapter 8). Automating runs the risk of categories becoming stale and no longer helpful.

A large part of the purpose of AI-based solutions is to save time and effort. When the manual effort amounts to ten minutes a day, giving up the benefits of AI-driven time-tracking, even at its theoretical optimum, is no great sacrifice.

Adoption

As a founder, you need to be fully comfortable with whatever you are recommending to your staff. If you have not tracked time before, there is an initial hill to climb when you first begin to measure your own productivity.

Many of us live under the illusion that we work eight hours a day, often more. The reality is that we are roughly half as productive as we think, and this can initially be a tough realization to come to terms with.

If a founder or firm does abandon the practice of time-tracking, it may well be due to a lack of comfort in dealing with the reality of how they do business. Hourly firms cannot afford this level of comfort. And in our humble opinion, any business, hourly or not, is better off confronting reality, since reality will eventually catch up in any case.

> "Many of us live under the illusion that we work eight hours a day, often more."

Rolling out with Staff

This brings us to the final topic, which weighs on the minds of many owners. How to get staff to buy in? If they have come from other firms, they may not be used to the idea of tracking time and may find it intimidating.

This intimidation factor is a genuine barrier, albeit a psychological one. It stems largely from misconceptions about how onerous and invasive the process will be, rather than from the actual experience of time-tracking, which thousands of professionals are carrying out every day.

One way of addressing these misconceptions is to get them out in the open. If you encourage people to voice what they think the challenges will be, you will be acknowledging these fears as well as being in a position to dispel them.

The two typical objections raised are that tracking time is intrusive ("Don't you trust us?") and impractical ("We should be focusing on our work."). Hiding beneath the first objection is a fear that the aim of the initiative is to ramp up the level of control and create a surveillance culture where everyone is being judged at all times.

But if you have followed the steps in the sections discussed earlier, you will have ensured the following:

- The staff have played (and will continue to play) an active role in defining and developing the categories.
- The number of categories is manageable.
- People know why we are tracking time and have a vested interest in achieving the underlying objectives.

As far as the impractical objection is concerned, the founder could begin with a trial period. The team will agree on some short-term objectives (for example, a target allocation as a group) and engage with the system wholeheartedly for a month. If, at the end of four weeks, everyone has survived, this will disprove the idea that time-tracking "just can't be done."

Furthermore, by this stage, the initial hill will have been climbed, and the habit should be formed. As with all innovations, the hardest part is getting from zero to one. By the time the review meeting comes around, there should be a genuine sense of curiosity as to how the final numbers have turned out in relation to what was planned or expected.

If this meeting goes well, it will be hard to argue against continuing to track time either on grounds of rationale or feasibility. People may well come to appreciate the clarity it brings to their working day.

These final three chapters have aimed to give guidance on the practical aspects of running an hourly firm. We hope that two truths are by now obvious: one, everything should be dynamic; and two, nothing is easy.

The unrelenting need for self-scrutiny at all levels is a source of difficulty, but also the source of the dynamism that drives the firm to become better.

The lessons we have written about are the fruits of many years of experimentation. As more people adopt the hourly model, alternative and enhanced approaches will be added to the general storehouse of best practices for hourly practitioners.

Closing Words

Self-reflectiveness and self-discipline are two characteristics that have allowed the human race to progress from spear-hunting to quantum physics in a mere fraction of the time life has existed on earth.

We believe that similar forces will elevate financial planning from an industry to something more than a profession, perhaps to become *the* profession, which sits at the center of all the other professional fields that help clients achieve their goals.

We wish you all the best in building this new future and hope this book has been of some assistance.

Acknowledgments

Whatever else it may be, this book has not been written in hopes of making the *New York Times* best-seller list. It is very much a labor of love and has depended to a great extent on the time and generosity of like-minded planners and generous-hearted friends.

Mark would like to thank his wife, Cheryce, who has supported him in every way since their wedding 25 years ago. Specific to the writing of this book, she endured endless calls on trips and reading drafts at the beach as he tried to keep this project going; his parents, Howard and Sharon, who backed this effort twenty years ago with a small loan (paid back twelve months later) and have been regular cheerleaders ever since. He would also like to thank Jeff Chinery, a GA advisor who has served as his entire independent "board of directors" for the past two decades, for sharing his wisdom and encouragement over the years. And finally, thanks are due to his team at Timothy Financial (Hoan, Becky, Michael, Kara Beth, Lydia, Jacob, Charis, Brian, Luke, Andrew, Audrey, Mark, and Blake) who are the secret behind the firm's success.

Matthew would like to thank Bob Veres, whose role as a connector, mentor, and supporter has made his journey thus far possible, and delightful. He owes professional thanks to Jan Engelke, his long-suffering mentor in Europe and the Middle East, who helped him understand the link between strategy and implementation, and Hermann Simon, who founded the company that has shown the world so much about pricing. He would also like to thank his parents for the gift of idealism; Hang-jin Chang, whose friendship has been a bulwark against many vicissitudes; Robert Han, whose counsel has always been forthcoming in time of need; and Christopher Kavanagh, whose intellectual sparring has been a source of cheer and much-needed challenge over the years.

Special thanks are due to the planners and consultants who have taken the time to review the manuscript in its final stages: Feraud Calixte, Debbra Dillon, Nancy Dienes, Anton Diedericks, Rob Pyne, and Brett Davidson. This book has been written for innovators like you, and you are our heroes.

We would like to thank Sheryl Garrett, whose article in *Financial Planning* magazine in 2000 was a catalyst for starting Timothy Financial Counsel, and who was one of the first to explore hourly as a viable model in financial planning for serving clients.

We also wish to thank our stellar team who have taken this book from Google document to Amazon-worthy publication: Sandra Wendel, our editor who has helped us navigate the self-publishing maelstrom; Laura Duffy, our cover designer, whose creativity and patience have saved us from a minefield of potential visual cliches; Megan McCullough for her expert interior design; Zack Washburn for his careful work checking the numbers; and our proofreader Mary Anne Shepard for getting us over the line.

Finally, we would like to offer thanks and encouragement to all who purchase, appreciate, and learn from this book. We look forward to seeing how the model alters and develops over the years through dialogue with practitioners who are living the hourly ideal.

About the Authors

Mark Berg

Mark Berg has been a fee-only financial counselor since 1995. He founded Timothy Financial Counsel, Inc., in 2000, which has since grown to become the largest fee-only, hourly-only financial planning firm in the United States. The Chicago-based firm has received multiple awards, including being recognized by AdvisoryHQ as among the Best Chicago Financial Advisors & Wealth Management Firms from 2015 to 2021.

Mark is passionate about financial planning, best seen in his volunteer work through the National Association of Personal Financial Advisors (NAPFA) where he has served on both the regional and national boards and has sat on several committees, and provided mentorship for other advisors. Mark serves on both nonprofit and for-profit boards.

In addition to participating as a speaker and panelist at conferences held by NAPFA, the AICPA, and the FPA, Mark has been quoted by a variety of publications, such as *Forbes*, *Crain's Chicago Business*, Dow Jones Newswires, *Wall Street Journal*, *Kiplinger's*, *Chicago Tribune*, *Reader's Digest*, and *Consumer Reports*. He has also been interviewed by ABC 7 News and NBC television, as well as having been a guest expert on the *Money Show* on WGN.

He holds a bachelor's degree in economics from Wheaton College and is a CFP® professional. Mark and his wife, Cheryce, live in Wheaton, Illinois, and have three sons, Joshua, Ryan (Jacki), and Luke.

Matthew Jackson

Matthew Jackson began his consulting career in 2006, working on a variety of strategy, technology, and M&A–related projects across multiple industries. His career has included six years at Simon-Kucher & Partners, the world's leading pricing consultancy, where he worked with teams in Europe, the Middle East, and North America to help clients navigate value proposition and pricing issues.

Since focusing on the field of financial advice full-time, he has authored numerous articles and white papers on the topic of pricing in financial advice and has been invited to speak at the AICPA, the Bob Veres Insider Forum, NAPFA, CFA Society, and the Trust Management Association.

In 2019 he founded Dialektic, a consultancy that helps financial advice firms prepare for disruption through adaptive strategies. This work has included new approaches to proposition design, compensation systems, pricing structures, and operations management. He began working with Mark Berg on the current book in the summer of 2020.

He holds a degree in classics from Oxford University and has held the Chartered Financial Analyst® designation since 2015. He lives in South Korea and works globally.